BENJAMIN BE

Lenten Mission
mar. 17- 20th '13

TUCKED
in the
ROCKS:

LIFE LESSONS *from the*
LAND *of* ENCHANTMENT

outskirtspress
DENVER, COLORADO

The opinions expressed in this manuscript are solely the opinions of the author and do not represent the opinions or thoughts of the publisher. The author has represented and warranted full ownership and/or legal right to publish all the materials in this book.

Tucked in the Rocks:
Life Lessons from the Land of Enchantment
All Rights Reserved.
Copyright © 2012 Benjamin Berinti, C.Pp.S.
v3.0

Cover Photo © 2012 JupiterImages Corporation. All rights reserved - used with permission.

This book may not be reproduced, transmitted, or stored in whole or in part by any means, including graphic, electronic, or mechanical without the express written consent of the publisher except in the case of brief quotations embodied in critical articles and reviews.

Outskirts Press, Inc.
http://www.outskirtspress.com

ISBN: 978-1-4327-9845-1

Outskirts Press and the "OP" logo are trademarks belonging to Outskirts Press, Inc.

PRINTED IN THE UNITED STATES OF AMERICA

*In loving memory of my grandmother Emma and
my godmother Frances, two women who taught me
many life lessons and who fed my imagination*

Table of Contents

Acknowledgements vii
    Tucked In Rock ix

The Prelude:
    Entering The Geography of The Land of Enchantment 1
    An Invitation 3
    The Sirens' Call 5
    On Being "Arrested" 9
    "The Language Of The Flowers" 15
    "Going In Circles" Isn't So Bad After All! 23

Life Lessons:
    "Sometimes In Order To See What's Right Here,
    You Have To Get Up And Go Over There" 27
    "Despite What Our Mothers May Have Taught Us,
    It Is Good To Stare" 36
    "It's Much Easier To See Through A Window Than A Door" ... 41
    "In Order To Soar With The Spirit,
    You Must First Get To The Bottom" 47
    "When Face To Face With Mystery,
    It's Best Not To Grab It" 53
        Poetic Interlude 58
    "Every Pearl Always Starts As A Pain-In-The-Shell" 60
    "Sometimes You Get To The Door,
    But You Can't Go Through" 71

"If You Want To Make A Change,
You May Need To Tell A Different Story"................................79
"When Everyone Is Looking For You,
Sometimes It's Best To Run The Other Way!" 89
"In The Menagerie Of Life, God Is No Kitten" 99
    Poetic Interlude 104
"In Order To See The Stars, You Have To Look Up!" 107
"In The Fabric Of Life, There Are Always Loose Threads"......113
"No Matter Where You Go,
Somebody's Been There Already"...124
"If The Clay's Not Moist, You Can't Throw The Pot" 130
"Every Majestic, Soaring Mountain Springs
From A Stressful Eruption Down Below" 139

Beyond The Land Of Enchantment:
    Living the Lessons Every Day..146
    While Waiting For My Baggage To Come 147

Postscript...151

Acknowledgements

"When one stands before any kind of art, it should tell nothing. It should, however, create the infinity of questions begetting questions."
(Artist Frank Howell)

It is certainly presumptuous on my part to suggest the words that follow are by any stretch of the imagination "art." However, whatever they may or may not be, they clearly emerge from questions in my own heart, and I desire that they give birth to questions in yours.

As a minister of the Word of God, I often meet people who, intending to be complimentary, tell me after a speaking engagement or Sunday homily: "I wish I had it figured out in my life as well as it sounds like you do in your life." They seem to believe because I deliver the Word, I must be secure in the Word and understand how it all fits together. Despite their good intentions, they are mistaken! And I tell them so. It is far easier to craft a reflection or homily than it is to live into them.

However, I do share this truth with them (after thanking them for their kindness to me). In everything I proclaim, I am not asking people to live or believe in something I am not wrestling with myself. At the heart of what may sound like "having it all together" can still be found the rumblings and questions of my own journey of faith.

I embrace the walk of Christian discipleship as an art, and therefore it often creates the infinity of questions Frank Howell suggests. Yet the reality of the questions by no means is a fearful thing for me, for these are questions wrapped in faith, in the love and grace of God who allows us room to come to know this God.

Art and questions have been sustaining gifts in my own life, and I owe this sustenance to many people. As you are about to begin this meditation on *Life Lessons from the Land of Enchantment*, I'd like to acknowledge a few of those influences.

I am grateful to my parents and to the Missionaries of the Precious Blood—my family. I am grateful for the Norbertine community of Santa Maria de la Vid in Albuquerque, New Mexico, whose hermitage retreat has provided the womb for many of these lessons to gestate. I am grateful for the opportunities I have had to encounter the great cultures of some of the pueblo peoples of New Mexico, who have reinforced my belief in the length, and breadth, and height and depth of God's presence in the world. I pray for the preservation and thriving of their ways of life and values amidst much in history and the present that conspire against them.

I am grateful for three former mentors at Saint Joseph's College in Rensselaer, Indiana, who nurtured in me a love for the power of words and the crafts of critical thinking and writing: Rev. Al Druhman, C.Pp.S., Dr. John Nichols, and Professor John Groppe. I am also grateful for the pastoral staff of the San Pedro Spiritual Development Center in the Diocese of Orlando for supporting me and allowing me to engage in the ministry of Word and Sacrament in such a sacred and enchanting place.

Tucked In Rock

"I love you, O Lord, my strength."

The print I leave, a passing mark
Now etched, quickly blown
Away
As the desert wrestles with the
Evening breath through
Mountain nostrils blown.

But I take heart, in my
Downward gaze,
In prints that remain,
Forgotten
Now remembered.

"The Lord is my rock in whom I take refuge."

I bend and stoop beneath the now
Raging sun, and hunt these specks and sparks
That shimmer
Against the pale dust;
And I recall…

"The Voice of the Lord shakes the wilderness."

For then the earth reeled and rocked,
The foundation-feet of mountains trembled
And quaked…

*And fire burst forth in flame-thrown
Coals,
Shooting, oozing, running red-hot-river.*

*Taken now, these precious jewels,
In reverent, tender hand,
Again the Voice beckons,
Through lips hot to cut and purge,
But gentle, too.
The Voice now tucked in these rocks.
They speak to me, like shells
Strewn so generously,
As treasure-gifts meted out
In pale grains of ocean shores.*

*Indeed, there is a Voice tucked in
These rocks of ages past,
Yet present.
Survivors they are, but worn and
Hidden
Until…*

"Yahweh's Voice convulses the desert."
"I love you, O Lord, my strength."

*Benjamin Berinti
Santa Maria de la Vid
Albuquerque, NM
September 8, 2003*

The Prelude: ENTERING THE GEOGRAPHY OF *THE LAND OF ENCHANTMENT*

*"I will lure her into the desert and
speak tenderly to her there"
(Hosea 2:4)*

*"Oh that the desert were my dwelling place,
with only fair spirit for my minister.
That I might forget the human race,
And hating no one, love her only."
(Lord Byron)*

*"And always there are mysteries in the desert,
stories told and retold of secret places in the
desert mountains...."
(John Steinbeck)*

An Invitation

"The desert is fertile!" With these bold words of Dom Helder Camara, the inspirational Brazilian bishop, echoing in my mind and heart, I sit amidst the fertile desert of the southwest mesa of Albuquerque, shadowed by the Sandia and Manzano mountain ranges, cradled by the spirit of the Norbertine community of Santa Maria de la Vid. This has been sacred ground for me for over 7 years, as I have traveled here for personal retreats. Immersed as I am in the ministry of offering retreats and renewal, it is all the more critical that I create the time and space to be on the receiving end of Sabbath time in my own prayer and reflection.

Like so many others who come to the lands of New Mexico, it doesn't take long to understand why the motto of this beautiful state is *The Land of Enchantment*. I believe God lured me to this desert place many years ago in order to speak tenderly to me. And one thing we know for certain about the God of all creation is that God is ever faithful to God's word.

I extend an invitation to all who take hold of these pages to enter into an experience of Sabbath and reflection, even if it lasts only the time it takes to get from the opening line of a chapter to its conclusion, from one paragraph to another.

"Tucked in the rocks" of this sacred place, the desert is indeed fertile because it is imbued with the presence of the God of the Sabbath, who calls out to each of us with an alluring voice, and who desires nothing more or less than abundant, flourishing life—even when our current surroundings may lead us to believe that no life is possible, let alone one that flourishes. The desert is indeed fertile, and its landscape simply *enchanting*!

What lies ahead of you along the journey of this book are "Life Lessons" from this *Land of Enchantment*. They are vignettes of experiences and encounters with God that have occurred over the years I have traveled here. Each life lesson emerges from either a specific encounter, or in some cases, the melding of several experiences into one shimmering stone that speaks truth for our life journey.

But before we set forth in reflection upon any particular life lesson, I invite you to first immerse yourself in the spirit of this *Land of Enchantment*, to taste a bit of what this sacred landscape calls forth, and to once again embrace the possibility that life can still be an *enchanting* experience, if we but allow ourselves to be present and attentive to its voice.

The Sirens' Call

Among the many fascinating stories of Greek mythology, one of the most enduring is the tale of the *Sirens*. Created with the body of a bird and topped with a beautiful female head, they lived on a rocky island from which they lured mariners to their deaths through the intoxicating charm of their songs. Promising the nearly irresistible gifts of knowledge, wisdom and a quickened spirit, their dulcet tunes traveled from ears to hearts like wildfire, only to leave the wreckage of lost lives strewn along the shores of their treacherous island. The famed Greek traveler Odysseus had to be lashed to the mast of his ship so as not to succumb to the *Sirens'* enticements (his crewmates had their ears stuffed with wax).

There are places and peoples who, with their own particular style of wooing, can draw us into their magic and promises. Some may, in truth, be as treacherous and deceptive as the *Sirens*, offering us false hopes and dreams hidden in the sweetly-spun sugar of cotton candy allure. Then there are other places and peoples whose mysterious magnetism is real, uplifting, challenging, nurturing, and draws us into a side of life we may too often neglect, or fear, or have little time for.

Considering the many magically musical tunes that have sailed from my ear to my heart over the years, I have concluded that the American Southwest may very well be populated with *Sirens*, as far as I can tell. For many years, only my imagination allowed me to enjoy and revel in the allurements of this wonderfully picturesque and colorful area of the United States…until at last I finally broke free of simple mind-pictures, and made my first voyage to New Mexico. It was love at first sight, first breath, and first deep encounter with the various Native peoples whose beauty of heart, culture, life, and loves abounds nearly as much as does the dramatic landscape itself. Indeed, as New Mexico calls itself, the *Land of Enchantment* has enchanted me so thoroughly, so completely, that I have made pilgrimage there nearly every year since (and sometimes, with good fortune, more than once per year).

Without a doubt, this *Land of Enchantment*, with its captivating *Sirens* calling out from artful arêtes, snaking rivers, majestic mesas, ancient stone-carved petroglyphs, deep-dwelling kivas, confounding cliff dwellings, native drumming circles, and eerily melodious flutes, offers up no misguided allurements nor destructive enticements, but rather overflows with life-giving refreshment and renewal.

I wonder how and where, in the course of each of our lives, we learn to take the necessary precautions that shield us from the all-too prominent *Sirens* that, despite the dripping sugar of their songs, desire nothing more than our ruin. With the songs of self-interest, self-aggrandizement, and self-centeredness being sung from every corner of our world and culture, how and where do we hear a different tune that turns us more radically away from our disheartening self-occupation *toward* a more healthy embrace of the common good, the care and concern of others so central to not only a truly vibrant and balanced personal life, but as importantly, a vibrant and balanced public life?

How and where do we open our ears to the call that will set us free, rather than lead to the demise of our very souls? Perhaps we may try, as did Odysseus' shipmates, to stuff our ears with "wax" to block out the undesirable tunes that come our way. Perhaps we try the old trick of our youth, where we shutter our ears and shout our "la-la-las" to overpower the sounds that would leave us bereft, tossed upon some dangerous shore.

Or perhaps, we are crazy enough to embrace a tiny whispering sound heard at the edge of our life-cave, or we stumble toward the alluringly tender tune rising from our deserts. Perhaps we cling to the Word made Flesh...whose voice lilts with the sweetest, most caring tones...and which invites us to the fullness of life and love.

The sheep hear his voice. He calls his own sheep by name and leads them out. The sheep follow him because they know his voice (John 10:3-5 NRSV).

But in order to hear the Good Shepherd, the *Siren-Son* of God, we must place ourselves in close proximity to his voice. We must sail often toward the shores of his resounding, yet gentle songs—especially in the community of the Church, where Jesus Christ promises he will always be present and speaking to us. If we feel, or have experienced one too many crashes along the rocks of the islands of despair, destruction, depression, and disappointment, maybe it indicates a need for a change of course, a journey that plants us in the middle of the goodness and gracious of the voice of the Lord rather than in the middle of allurements and enticements that lead to broken hearts, souls and relationships.

The world in which we live, like the deadly *Sirens* of ancient mythology, seems focused more upon the *allurement* itself than the end results. So often we are lured by advertising, false hopes and promises, charlatans who manipulate, unfounded guarantees, physical enhancements, and myriad superficial bonuses—all playing most often to our deepest insecurities. Then once we are "caught," there is no concern about what happens to us next. We are left to wallow and fend for ourselves, beaten, damaged and disappointed, until another *new and improved* intoxicating, melodic allure comes our way.

The voice of Jesus Christ not only draws us in…but keeps us sustained through whatever joys and sorrows come our way—whether those of our choosing, or those that lay hold of us despite our best resistance.

We all need people and places whose *voices* draw us to life…and not to death (in its many forms). Many times, God uses the beauty and majesty of God's creation; the history and art of peoples; the music and culture of ancient wisdoms to lure us in.

To what shores are the *Sirens* drawing you these days? To whose music are you attending? How often do you sail close enough to hear the gentle, humble, yet authoritative voice of the Son of God?

On Being "Arrested"

Two unrelated incidents occurred to me in the same week that brought my attention to the "long arm of the law" and led me to some back door insights. While in flight heading toward my annual retreat with the Norbertine community of Santa Maria de la Vid in New Mexico, I was troubling over a recent development with the Orlando diocesan fingerprint/background check policy that our parish had just begun to implement days before my departure. The other incident, one making national news, was the splash that former Dallas Cowboys football coach Barry Switzer made when he was detained by law enforcement officials at an airport for carrying a pistol in his luggage (sandwiched, I suppose between his tooth paste and deodorant stick)! Now Barry, while thoroughly ensconced on the ornery side of the personality scale, simply made a bonafide, major league, bone-headed, worthy-of-American-sports mistake (and wonderful fodder for the always starving and incessant 24-7 sports news cycle on television)—no two ways about it! And as is so often the case in our bizarre media culture, we all received more than enough "news" about Mr. Switzer's dilemma. What difference it really made, as I was whisking through my own bag scan at the security checkpoint at Orlando International, I'm not really sure. But then again, since when has making a real difference been part of getting oneself into the headlines?

Closer to home, and not quite so dramatic, many parishioners had been lamenting the first weekend of fingerprint process implementation. It was the first time in my own life I had ever been fingerprinted, and at first, it left me with a somewhat eerie feeling. Clearly, I am convinced of its necessity as part of the ongoing efforts of the Church to lay a foundation for safe environments for all those who come to us and participate in our life, but I must admit that the actual experience was disconcerting, to say the least. (Although I have to say, sticking my hands into that ink-cleaning goop afterwards was kind of fun!) After the inking was completed, and my card had been placed in the stack with countless others, I had a wave of relief and thankfulness pass over me. I was thankful that I was being fingerprinted for *this* particular purpose—and *not* because I was about to be sent to the slammer. You know…ARRESTED!

So how do these things come together now? As the images and feelings of what it must be like to really be arrested floated in and out of my mind during the tedious flight at 33,000 feet, I found myself saying: "thank you…no!" There are some things in life *not* worth experiencing—even if it means owning up to your closest companions, during one of those late night, feeling good, shooting the breeze, Paul Bunyon-esque kinds of conversations, that you *have not* ever been arrested and have never experienced life "on the inside." Sorry guys, never been to the joint! The only "time" I've ever done was when I had to sit through someone's 4-hour vacation video from a Disney cruise! That was punishment enough for me!

However, as I rolled through those words and the experience of *being arrested,* I began to realize that in fact, *I have been arrested,*

On Being "Arrested"

on numerous occasions, and was about to repeat that experience once I landed in *The Land of Enchantment* and made my way to the sacred grounds of the retreat center and my spirit-filled hermitage for the next 5 days. And on top of all that…I did, in fact, grow and prosper from those experiences!

Now before anyone runs out and tries to claim a weighty cash reward from *America's Most Wanted* by turning me in for an outstanding warrant or two, let me explain more clearly!

In a discussion of *living artfully* in his book *Care of the Soul (Harper Perenniel, 1994, 286)*, Thomas Moore has this to say:

> *The emptiness that many people complain dominates their lives comes in part from a failure to let the world in, to perceive it and engage it fully. Naturally, we'll feel empty if everything we do slides past without sticking. Soul cannot thrive in a fast-paced life because being affected, taking things in and chewing on them, requires time. Living artfully, therefore, might require something as simple as pausing. Some people are incapable of* **being arrested** *[my emphasis] by things because they are always on the move.*

Yes indeed, we who live the fast-paced life in the 21st century, rarely have time to decelerate and allow ourselves to *be arrested by* the world that surrounds us. In Thomas Moore's view, we cannot really claim to be *living* if we do not allow ourselves to *live with* the world that surrounds us, to truly both engage it and to be engaged by it. Indeed, living artfully requires that we allow the relationships, the observations, the impressions of daily living to sink in, to penetrate to the level of our souls. The vitality of our lives does depend upon whether we allow the world to continue to pass by us, at an ever increasingly rapid clip, or whether we allow ourselves to *be arrested by,* literally grabbed by and held by the encounters of our daily living. So often, we simply try to "make it through" any given day (and for some, that in itself takes all the attentiveness they can muster), never stopping long enough, never pausing or lingering over *where*, in fact, we happen to be going, nor to determine the nature of the *what* we are so desperately trying to "make it through."

The same problem infects our ability to worship and pray each Sunday, the Lord's Day for Sabbath. Too often, we cannot be arrested by God during worship or the Eucharist because we're just sliding through, distracted, wondering about our next move, trying to see who is and who isn't going to communion, or who isn't dressed the way we think they should be.

Has the *long arm of God* reached out to arrest you lately? Can you identify some experience in the past week that *arrested* your attention—a person, place or object; some encounter that made you pause; something that grabbed you as you navigated the twists and turns of your life's path? Was there really anything to "chew on," as Moore suggests, something dropped on your plate you didn't even notice?

I know that when I am arrested by someone or something, I can literally be stopped dead in my tracks and be transported to a different place, a moment almost out of time, a deeper level of living—even if it is only a momentary diversion. Of course, these experiences would be, could be more than flashes or glimpses of artful living IF I were to slow down enough to be arrested more often, if I could develop a *habit* of being arrested.

I have had the occasion to be arrested by something as

On Being "Arrested"

simple as a squirrel, cautiously moving round and round one of the trees towering between my front door and the sidewalk (and watching that same squirrel plot some way of scaling the pole now holding a cache of sunflowers seeds intended for waiting cardinals—*not* squirrels). When I paused and allowed myself to be caught up in the squirrel's movement, that kind of hide-and-seek game it plays, I was transported to an image of how God seems to work in my life. At times, I really feel I'm playing a hide-and-seek game with God, and sometimes, God is doing that with me! Like the squirrel, every time one moves in for a closer look, God seems to move to the "other side"—just beyond my view.

The sound of heavy thunder peals one night arrested my attention, and I was moved to feel the forceful power of nature that surrounds me. The cry of children outside my window one evening arrested my attention, and I was taken back to a time when my friends and I used to hang out on late, sultry sunlit summer nights, and played "freeze-defrost" running through each others' front yards. I was arrested by the smell of the candles when they were extinguished one morning after Mass, and I was reminded of how much I love that smell and how it invites me to feel closeness to holy things, and how I am thankful that God chooses to give us tangible ways to know and experience and love God. I was arrested by the tragic sound of squealing tires as an accident was occurring…a beautiful ray of light coming through a stained glass window…the half-joyful/half-frightened smile of a soon-to-be Pre-Kindergarten student in school…the tender way a father was cradling his 3-year-old at donut time following a Sunday liturgy.

As the writer and spiritual guide Evelyn Underhill so wisely proclaimed: ***For lack of attention, a thousand forms of loveliness elude us every day.***

Certainly, you can name your own encounters, can't you? Maybe it's not so bad, after all, getting this kind of *arrested*. It does have its upside! A rap sheet filled with people and experiences that draw us more deeply into life would be a proud record to flaunt. *Being arrested* on a regular basis is the key to discovering many hidden *life lessons tucked in the rocks*.

"The Language Of The Flowers"

> "Alice laughed: "There's no use trying," she said; "one can't believe impossible things."
> "I daresay you haven't had much practice," said the Queen. "When I was younger, I always did it for half an hour a day. Why, sometimes I've believed as many as six impossible things before breakfast."
> *(Alice in response to the White Queen, in Lewis Carroll's Through the Looking Glass)*

Believing impossible things—isn't that what part of *enchantment* is all about? Each time I descend from the clouds above the Albuquerque Sunport (speaking of what people for generations would have deemed maddeningly impossible), despite the dry, arid, adobe-parched landscape that comes into view, I am drawn immediately into a vivid and fertile landscape that is my imagination. Long before visiting New Mexico, thankfully, I found a home in an enchanted imagination through the magic of no less than Mr. Rogers!

Fred Rogers, *aka* "Mr. Rogers," was a part of my steady diet as a youngster growing up in Pittsburgh. His now famous children's program, with Mr. Rogers decked out in canvas boating sneakers and those nondescript sweaters, was produced at the local PBS outlet in my home town. Consequently, all Pittsburgh residents had a special affinity for Mr. Rogers. In those simple days before the creation of nursery schools, day cares, and VPKs, along with *Romper Room*, my earliest schooling came via *Mr. Rogers' Neighborhood*. While his lessons on self-esteem (of course, as a child watching the program, I hadn't the foggiest idea that my "self" was being "esteemed" through his methods!) and his admonitions about manners were quite instructive, it was really the daily trip made on the trolley to the "Village of Make-Believe" that was most engrossing. Perhaps more than anything, Fred Rogers instilled in children a great love for **imagination.** In his own way, simplistic by today's high-tech standards, he allowed children room to bring their own creative play and fantasy to his television show. In the somewhat Spartan setting of his television sound stage, there was room for me to *make-believe* on my own terms, using his scenes and characters as a backdrop. This is so much unlike many children's programs today where all the glitz and glitter leaves no room for one's own imagination. I suppose that, along with other influences, I can point to those days spent with King Friday, X the Owl, Lady Elaine, and all the other inhabitants of *Make-Believe*, as the source of my lifelong love of imagination—and what I now know to be its absolute necessity for a thriving life of Christian faith.

 My thoughts turn to Mr. Rogers and those primal beginnings of my attraction to cultivating the imagination as I enter this New Mexican *Land of Enchantment*—filled with its own characters and stories, waiting to be breathed into the landscape of the days of my upcoming retreat.

 As I wait my turn to be unpacked from the sardine can that has been our airliner for the past nearly four hours, I begin to muse over a scene that occurred just a few days ahead of my departure.

I had stopped by a parishioner's home and walked into the middle of some children recreating the May Crowning (of the Blessed Virgin Mary) they had experienced at the school Mass earlier that same day. Each of them was taking turns playing Mary, as well as sharing in the other roles of the day's liturgy. An ordinary towel, bathrobe, and various other items were transformed from their natural functions into a veil, a gown, a crown of flowers, and the other necessities to make the crowning complete. I marveled at the children's ability to make believe, to recreate through the power of their imaginations this wonderful ritual. This, to me, was *play* at its best! No whirling or beeping game toys, no celluloid icons, no computer graphics, no high-priced mechanics—just imagination!

As adults, we often forget the importance of cultivating imagination. We tend to think of its powers as being only within the domain of children. Somehow, we've come to believe that adulthood equals *seriousness* and childhood equals *playfulness*. As adults, we mistake imagination for flights of fancy that take us away from the *real* world. Yet, at one time, each of us in our own way was a practitioner of imaginative vision; we reveled in make-believe worlds that could occupy an entire day. Now, as adults, we call it *day dreaming*, and we convict ourselves of a felony when we find ourselves wandering into such dreamy trances—wasting time, is our charge. If we're not too harsh on ourselves, we may allow momentary imaginative diversions, but then we quickly get back to our *serious* pursuit of life's demands and constraints.

As we grow older our amazement at the wondrous quality of the world dims, our sense of awe, and intense apprehension, the keen taste of beauty and poignancy that can break us into tears—all that diminishes, writes Albert J. Raboteau.

Shel Silverstein, a noted author of children's literature, spoke of this wonderful capacity to imagine and of our struggle with its loss as adults, by referring to it as a *forgotten language*. In his book, *Where the Sidewalk Ends,* Silverstein writes:

> *Once I spoke the language of the flowers,*
> *Once I understood each word a caterpillar said,*
> *Once I smiled in secret at the gossip of the*
> *starlings,*
> *And shared a conversation with the housefly*
> *in my bed.*
> *Once I heard and answered all the questions of*
> *The crickets,*
> *And joined the crying of each falling dying flake*
> *Of snow,*
> *Once I spoke the language of the flowers...*
> *How did it go?*
> *How did it go?*

We often lose, or at least seriously misplace, our own ability to speak the *language of the flowers,* and we suffer because of this loss. Perhaps we don't make the connection, but it seems that to live our life of faith as Christians requires, even demands of us, a vibrant, healthy, and vigorous imagination. To nurture and be nurtured in our faith, we need our imaginations stimulated!

Maybe this talk of imagination strikes us as being *opposed* to faith. After all, don't we often assume that faith is about teachings, doctrines, truths, ritual practices and obligation—things that are set in concrete? Don't we often think that faith means holding on to something solid, less flighty? Even at times, I am afraid that we associate imagination and fantasy with *sin*—imagining things and people and situations that lead us away from God.

But what could be more wrought with imagination that Jesus' vision of the Kingdom of God? In fact, the bulk of Jesus' preaching, teaching and serving always required an exercise of imagination in one, simple way: people had to *see* something beyond what they were currently seeing; they had to imagine a reality that had not yet come to pass, whether in their own personal lives or in their society, but one in which they desperately wanted to share.

Yes, imagination is at the heart and soul of our faith in God. As Amos Wilder pleads in his book *Theopoetic: Theology and the Religious Imagination,* imagination is

> *a necessary component of all profound knowing and celebration.... It is at the level of imagination that any full engagement with life takes place.*

Wilder seems to be echoing those familiar words of Jesus when he tells us that at the core of his saving mission is that *we have life and have it in abundance!* If we are to experience this fullness of life, then it would seem that we must do so by engaging our imaginations.

One of the reasons that Jesus is so kind toward children, even to the point of scolding his disciples who try to prevent them from coming to him, is because he must have realized their innate capacity to imagine. In Jesus' words: *Let the children come to me; do not prevent them, for the kingdom of God belongs to such as these (Mark 10:14 NRSV).* Perhaps this is why faith seems to get much harder to exercise as we get older; perhaps as our capacity for imagination diminishes, whether through the stresses and strains of life, the gnawing disappointments and disillusionments (disenchantments) we experience, or simply our lack of attention to feeding it, our capacity for faith also diminishes. We too, like children, need to be able to envision that which does not yet exist in its completeness.

While much has been written by all sorts of specialists about the power of the imagination and how it works within people, one of the simplest definitions I have ever encountered about the nature of imagination is this: ***Imagination is the power/capacity to make absent things present.***

Isn't that what we find ourselves doing in our faith life? Don't we spend a lot of time in prayer and worship, in acts of compassion and love, trying to *make present* to ourselves and others things that seem absent? We offer love and understanding where only hurt and confusion seem to reign; we offer forgiveness where only bitterness and distrust reside; we offer comfort and hope where only sadness and despair are in control; we offer life where only death seems to call out. At every turn along the path of our journey of faith, we find ourselves constantly confronted with the need for exercising our ability to *see* what we find missing.

It seems to me that, if we were to make an addition to our sacred Christian creeds, we might want to insert these words of Maria Rainer Rilke, who wrote in his *Sonnets to Orpheus*:

> *But for us existence is still enchanted; still in a hundred places the source. A play of pure powers, touched only by those who kneel and wonder (Pt. II, no. 10).*

"The Language Of The Flowers"

Without a strong imagination, how can we even hope to come into relationship with this wildly generous, compassionate, forgiving, creative God whom Jesus reveals to us—this God of, as the poet Jessica Powers describes, *too much giving*? Is it any wonder that Jesus' primary teaching tool was the use of *parable*—all those "Once upon a time" worlds to which we only gain access through the gate of story? Without a rich imagination, how is it possible for Christians rooted in Eucharistic practice to maintain our belief that a single wafer of wheat and a trifling sip of wine are *truly* the Body and Blood of Christ, that body and blood which Jesus tells us in John's Gospel is *real* food and drink unto eternal life? Indeed, imagination is a necessary virtue to cultivate if we are to have a vibrant life of faith.

The poet Denise Levertov, in a 1984 essay entitled *A Poet's View*, shared this insight about the link between imagination and faith:

> *It must therefore be by the exercise of that faculty [imagination] that one moves toward faith, and possibly by its failure that one rejects it as delusion.*

Put another way by theologian Sally McFague, in her book *Metaphorical Theology*, disregarding our imagination makes it *more difficult, not impossible, for us to believe in our hearts what we confess with our lips.*

Without the power of holy imagination, without a source by which we have this God-given capacity nurtured, our faith can become dry, brittle, dulled and pathetic—not unlike the New Mexican landscape in the middle of prolonged drought. The marvelous *language* of our faith can quickly become another casualty, another *forgotten language of the flowers* if we don't find ways to have it nourished and sustained.

Elizabeth Barrett Browning, recalling God's invitation to Moses to approach the burning bush, writes:

> *The earth is ablaze with the fire of God, but only those who see it take their shoes off. The rest sit around and pick blackberries.*

Life may indeed be serious business, but it is not livable, it is not sustainable without periodic ventures into the open spaces and unlimited visions that are created when we allow the power of imagination to transport us to our own *lands of enchantment*, wherever they may be. Perhaps we all need to find our own little Mr. Rogers' trolley to carry us away into that fertile land of enchantment where our encounter with God can come alive!

"Going In Circles" Isn't So Bad After All!

I'm sure many of us have used the expression, "I feel like I'm going in circles" on more than one occasion. Perhaps these very words were on our lips today before cracking open this page! Generally, we don't utter this phrase to indicate something positive; rather we use it in a pejorative way. It's our shorthand way to indicate that we seem to be stuck, going nowhere in particular, expending a lot of energy with little to show in return for our investment. If we are "going in circles," our greatest desire usually is to "get back on track." In other words, we want to straighten ourselves out and move forward. Somehow we believe that progress and getting somewhere are accomplished when moving in a straight line. Our modern world view tends to see things in *linear* fashion. Problem is…the world isn't linear—literally or figuratively!

"Going in circles" is the way that many people throughout history have viewed the very essence of life's movement. In this particular way of seeing and living, anything and everything worth doing is worth doing in circles! While New Agers have their crystals and belief in pyramid-power, the **circle** has been a source of power for eons. For most of our ancestors, anything worth doing was worth doing in circles.

[Handwritten margin notes: Trinity is a circle / our birth leads eventually back to our Creator thru death & resurrection; learn & lived thru faith]

Tucked in the Rocks

Heháka Sápa (translated "Black Elk"), a Native American Oglala Lakota (Sioux) Elder, has this to say:

> *You have noticed everything an Indian does is in a circle, and that is because the Power of the World always works in circles, and everything tries to be round. The Wind, in its greatest power whirls. Birds make their nests in circles…the sun comes forth and goes down again in a circle. The Moon does the same, and both are round. The life of man is a circle from childhood to childhood, and so it is in everything where power moves.*

Anything worth doing is worth doing in circles! For we who are Christian people, we too move in circles—circles of fellowship, of communion, of death and resurrection. Our liturgical life is guided by circular seasons; cycles of sacred scriptures we read and break open; ritual movements also capture our fundamental belief that God's movements are circular. Too often we have mistakenly envisioned God as Trinity in the symbolic form of a pyramid or triangle (somehow this seemed to provide a clearer basis for modeling the Church in a pyramidal structure). Yet when we contemplate the wonder and beauty of the unfathomable mystery of God as Trinity—we are better served by envisioning the essence of Father, Son and Spirit as fundamentally a circle of relationship, from which all life springs and within which all life is nurtured and sustained.

Perhaps this vision is no more beautifully and faithfully captured than in the incredible icon of the Trinity attributed to Andrei Rublev (c. 1410), wherein the three angels who visited

"Going In Circles" Isn't So Bad After All!

Abraham and Sarah at the Oak of Mamre, gather around a table in circular symmetry, while leaving open a space and gesturing for anyone who looks upon them, to join their circle of love and relationship.

Life looks, feels and "lives" differently when we are "going in circles." Perhaps the daily rush forward that seems to wear upon us, perhaps the drive to "keep on track" that we believe to be so important for maintaining our life are really distractions from the *real* direction and movement we might best pursue.

Indeed we spring forth, in the words of the theme song from *The Lion King*, from the *"circle of life."* And for those of us who claim the name Christian, this is no figurative, whimsical metaphor—for indeed, we spring from THE circle of life, the blessed Trinity of Father, Son and Holy Spirit!

In a practical way, I suggest this might now be a way, a path through the series of life lessons that are about to unfold. The life lessons in these pages are purposely not listed as numerical, chronologically identified chapters. That's too linear! While the book could not be printed in a circular format (and you might be too befuddled if we skipped numbering the individual pages), it doesn't mean the reader cannot still approach the pages in just such a way.

What I'm suggesting is this…after immersing yourself in the *Prelude* (and don't be afraid to return to it many times), and now ready to embark on the Life Lessons, feel free to do so "out of order." Feel free to jump the track and weave your way in and out of the lessons. Perhaps, you may even want to really be bold and to read portions of one life lesson, and before completing it, spin your way into another. You may be surprised that while each lesson is self-contained, the wisdom God reveals in each of them, can be woven into a wonderful tapestry, a fabric of many colors.

Whirl your way, like the wind, through one lesson and then another; circle back and recapture the insights of one lesson after having tasted another's wisdom. And if you find your head and heart spinning, going in circles by what you read…then I will have been blessed in my efforts here.

Life Lesson:

"Sometimes In Order To See What's Right Here, You Have To Get Up And Go Over There"

"SOMETIMES IN ORDER TO SEE WHAT'S RIGHT HERE, YOU HAVE TO GET UP AND GO OVER THERE"

Twenty four hours ago it was a sprawling desert and soaring mountain peaks. Now it is a humid breeze and the Atlantic Ocean at sea level. Twenty four hours ago it was jackrabbits darting across the dusty trails. Now it is a bevy of banana spiders clinging sternly to their massive webs amidst the sea grapes. Twenty four hours ago it was sage brush and tumbleweed. Now it is cabbage and date palms rustling their fanned plumes. Twenty four hours ago, I was in the high desert of the south valley of Albuquerque; today I am in New Smyrna Beach.

The physical changes in the landscape are baffling and a bit unnerving to me now. *That* was "retreat"; *this* is "home." Yet, somehow, the physical world around me opens a window at a deeper level. Part of it is simply the re-entry phase of "connecting" again after eight days of near total silence and solitude; part of it is the jet-lag, coupled with an after-midnight arrival home and now functioning on a few hours sleep. And all this in anticipation of what I'm about to begin.

Twenty four hours ago I was *on* retreat; twenty four hours later, I am the one *giving* a retreat — to the Franciscan friars working in the Diocese of Orlando.

"Sometimes In Order To See What's Right Here, You Have To Get Up And Go Over There"

As I gaze out now at the gently rolling waters of the Atlantic, under an equally bright and glorious sun as I had experienced in New Mexico (although, without the raging humidity of today), a scene ever so different from where I have just come, a minor revelation emerges for me. Or perhaps better said, I am *reminded* of a simple but profound truth: **changes in the landscape reflect the changes in our souls.**

And because of this truth, it has become clear to me that *sometimes in order to see what's right here in front of me, I need to get up and go over there.*

There are deep feelings and emotions which accompany me now as I look out on water instead of parched, dusty trails; as I look upon a congregation of fair-skinned sun worshippers trying to bronze themselves instead of naturally bronzed and fire-red skinned Native Americans; as I look out across an uninterrupted horizon instead of miles of geological wonder arching skyward to over 10,000 feet. Changes in landscape can be reflective of changes in our souls — but we don't have to *travel* to see or notice them. Sometimes, from the comfort (or discomfort) of our own Lazy Boy recliner, or from the swing in our backyard, or in front of the computer terminal at work, or an hour of prayer at Sunday Mass — we can traverse a vast array of landscapes. And in doing so, we find a way to unveil that which has been hidden from us because we've been stuck in one place, trying to gain insight without ever moving, wrestling with the same demons in the same arena. Ultimately, our myopia leaves us incapable of really seeing what's "right here," what's right in front of us.

Sometimes, we too are soaring high above the plains, lofty in our thoughts, hopes and dreams for the present or future. Like Peter, James and John, who were graced with the Transfiguration of Jesus, and who desired to never set foot beyond that hallowed ground: "Lord," Peter asks (begs?), "should we set up camp here?" we too long for "peak experiences" that lift us from the hardships of life on the ground. Sometimes, the power of love in our lives is so strong, so clear, so nurturing, that we believe we have been lifted high on eagles' wings and are coasting above the heartaches and pains of daily living, seeing sights through the eyes of a lover that we've never seen.

Sometimes, we find our lives arid and parched, thirsting for hope, joy, confidence, and renewed spirit like the cracked and pock-marked face of the desert. Like the psalmists, we wonder, "How long, O Lord, will we be wandering in the wilderness?" All the plans we have made, worked so hard at achieving, can come crashing down with the sudden death of a loved one, the loss of our job, the illness of a child, a son or daughter called off to war, a slump into depression.

Sometimes, we are "on the level," and we can see our lives with a clarity that simply allows us to accept ourselves and others "where we are." We have that quiet confidence and trust that God does prevail in all things, and we need not look for God majestically seated on some lofty throne above us, nor buried beyond our sight. We experience God to be *here*, where we are, close to us and as constant and repetitive as the waxing and waning of the tides.

Sometimes, as Hildegard of Bingen would say, we are *green*, that is, full of life and energy...ready to tackle the world with no one stopping us. Sometimes, we are harsh and drab, unwilling to grow and unwavering in our despair. Sometimes, we are firmly rooted and fearless in reaching beyond our present limitations; sometimes we are uprooted and tossed about the landscape like a dried ball of sage brush, pushed across a barren landscape,

"Sometimes In Order To See What's Right Here, You Have To Get Up And Go Over There"

heading nowhere in particular. Sometimes, we sway in the breeze with little care for what the new day might bring to us; sometimes, we are blown and buffeted by unfriendly surges which toss us about and make our heads and hearts adrift with confusion and doubt.

Yes, changes in landscape can be mirrors of changes in our souls. There are, to say correctly, **landscapes within our souls,** and we can refuse to budge from where we are, no matter how intriguing or inviting a "change of scenery" might be for us. There are days when we welcome a new view, a new look at the world around us and our relationships, and there are those days when even the threat of illness or long-term debilitation will not push us over the edge of the all-too-familiar territory we inhabit every day.

Perhaps the conundrum often is, the truth is we really *do not* desire the changes we claim, and we're quite frankly *not* really interested in seeing what is right in front of us.

The question before me now is: can I embrace this new landscape set before me? Can I hold on to the memories of where I have been, not forgetting the impressions and contours of that blessed space so many miles from here, while still entering fully into the land I now inhabit? How can I find the courage to finally *get up and go over there in order to really see what is right here*?

There are fearful hesitations too. How settled will I become once things return to "normal"? Will I lose my zest for adventure and exploration? Can I allow myself to be open to the many landscapes through which God will surely continue to guide me?

When we look at the Scriptures, particularly the journey in faith taken (and strayed from) by our ancestors in faith, the Hebrew-Israelite-Jewish peoples, we see a wide-ranging array of mountains and valleys, rivers and lakes, rocks and hills, desert and oasis, fertile crescents and barren wastelands through which they were led. And this is precisely the key — all the while, they were *being led…by a gracious and generous God, who remained faithful* in spite of unrelenting infidelity on the part of God's covenanted loved ones. But in order to become the people they were called to be, to fully respond to the invitation of God, who cajoled them at every twist and turn with God's words, *I am your God and you are my people*—they had to be on the move. They had to be a *pilgrim people*; they had to get up from where they had been and go to another place, only to return to the place where they began with new insight and wisdom and ownership of their true identity as a people claimed by God.

Jesus often invited his disciples to get up and move to an *out of the way place* in order to gain some distance on the places they'd been and the people to whom they had ministered. This distance allowed them the perspective of looking back from *there* from *out here*. This out of the way landscape was to provide not merely a respite or hiding place from daily struggles, but rather a landscape for revelation.

And the cartography of our own journey is not much different, nor is the gracious and generous faithfulness of a God who continues to lead, never leaving us abandoned, no matter the peak or valley we happen to occupy, no matter the terrain of our souls.

Back in the days of my college ministry at Saint Xavier University in Chicago, I worked with a wonderful team of Student Life personnel—people who were not only dedicated to their craft and the well-being of our students, but quite frankly, just people who were a lot of fun to be around, to go to work with every day (and lots of nights, too).

"Sometimes In Order To See What's Right Here, You Have To Get Up And Go Over There"

One of the characters with whom my partner in Campus Ministry and I worked closely was the Student Activities Director. While all of us had more than our fair share of daily student angst—everything from overdue papers, to lost loves, to tuition shortfalls, to imbibing too heavily the night before a final, to emotional meltdowns—Jimmy had extra doses of it!

Along the way, Jimmy coined what became a familiar clarion call to all of us in the office when a student or group of students were going off the deep end and exaggerating the length and depth of their current angst. In his words, the *Out of Proportion Club* was convening!

The reality that phrase captured for us then, and still carries meaning for me today, is that too often what is right before our eyes gets "out of proportion," and we can no longer see it or deal with it in a healthy way. While there may be many opportunities or strategies to restore "proportion" in our life, one seems to work better than others, and that is *to get up from here and go over there*—whether that means a literal moving from one space, one geography, one landscape to another, or whether that means imaginatively moving from one space, one geography, one landscape to another.

Paging through the journal from my retreat where this life lesson first began to percolate, I see how I posed the practical question: What does "back there" [my ministry and home] look like from "out here"? Allow me to share some of the entries that give evidence of the power of **getting up and going over there**, which perhaps may help give you a flavor of what a new vision can sound and look like in your own life.

"Back there" looks like where I call *home*, and "out here" is a place to *visit* (although there is an allure to New Mexico that could make it a home if my life situation were different). Places to visit are wonderful temporary homes, but they lack the depth of permanency. I see now that I need to more fully embrace "back there" as a true home, feeling a greater sense of ownership and belonging than I have allowed myself to feel for the past two years.

"Back there" looks less harsh and troublesome from "out here." I often allow my frustrations and disappointments to pull me down, and I sometimes project my issues and inadequacies onto the place and people—and then resent them for it. The vastness of this New Mexican landscape "out here" really makes "back there" look smaller, more manageable, less overwhelming in the grand scheme of all creation!

"Back there" looks like one small piece of a huge Church—that is as diverse as the heart of the Creator. Our parish "issues" may have some momentary importance, for a limited number of people, and they should not be ignored out of hand, but they are small and incredibly insignificant from "out here." "Out here" I see the results of untold millions of years of life and struggle—and so, "back there" is merely a drop of water in a vast ocean.

And yes, "back there" looks a bit dull from "out here." The breathtaking beauty of these natural (not "manufactured" a la Disney World) wonders make my home seem boring and flat. Even my great love for the seashore and tropical beauty "back there" seems challenged by what I see and experience "out here." This reminds me that there are more things I enjoy, love and value than what I allow myself to take part in "back there." Surrounded by the artistry and creativity of people "out here," I am challenged to connect with the artistry and creativity that also abounds "back there," but which I often neglect or don't spend the time seeking.

Twenty four hours ago it was a sprawling desert and soaring

"Sometimes In Order To See What's Right Here, You Have To Get Up And Go Over There"

mountain peaks. Now it is a humid breeze and the Atlantic Ocean at sea level. Twenty four hours ago it was jackrabbits darting across the dusty trails. Now it is a bevy of banana spiders clinging sternly to their massive webs amidst the sea grapes. Twenty four hours ago it was the sage brush and tumbleweed. Now it is the cabbage and date palms swaying in the wind. The transition between landscapes can be more than a bit unsettling, and I find myself today with mixed emotions as I cross from one land to another. Yet, I also stand before the breathtaking landscape upon which I gaze, and I gaze upon the boundless landscape within me with a sure and steady confidence that the "great cartographer," who allows us to make our own paths in this life, is keeping a steady eye and hand upon the map of my soul. I am also confident that this great God is doing the same for you!

And there is one more thing of which I am heartily convinced about this "map-making" God—that God, too, is a traveler, a sojourner, a mover and shaker, who never desires us to become so set in our landscape that we can no longer witness God's presence and invitation right before our eyes. No, this God gives living testimony to the lesson I've learned along the way, whether from the mountains of New Mexico to the shimmering waters of New Smyrna Beach, Florida, or from the journey from my head to my heart—*sometimes in order to see what's right here, you have to get up and go over there.*

Life Lesson:

"Despite What Our Mothers May Have Taught Us, It Is Good To Stare"

"Despite What Our Mothers May Have Taught Us, It Is Good To Stare"

Have you ever been busted "staring"? Not the kind where you are simply spaced out and looking at no one and nothing in particular. I mean caught in the act of definitely looking, with incredible focus and rapt attention at someone or something. If you have, I suspect your initial response is embarrassment or humiliation. Those of us who are quick on our feet (or should I say, quick with our eyes) may rapidly divert our gaze or muddle through some attempt to demonstrate that we were *not* staring at all.

It seems that one of those early "life lessons" that gets thrust upon us (along with "eat your spinach and get arms like Popeye") is "DON'T STARE! IT'S NOT POLITE!" I'm not sure why we assign such immoral dread to something that is, quite frankly, incredibly natural and perhaps holds a key to touching something deep within us.

When we stare at someone or something, it usually means we are giving what is being "observed" our fullest attention. Maybe that's what makes the whole thing discomforting. We are increasingly becoming accustomed to *ignoring* much of what happens around us, bidding little real attention to life as it unfolds, so perhaps these moments spent in utter attention and connection somehow seem unnatural.

During my years living in urban Chicago, there was an unwritten, though highly practiced, rule about exchanging eye contact with people on the streets of the city. I lived much of my time in Hyde Park, an area of the city near the University of Chicago that is known for its great cultural institutions, its dynamic urban life, and an incredible diversity of people. In fact, the local Catholic parish, St. Thomas the Apostle, had for many years proclaimed as their parish motto: "God's People in Extra-Ordinary Variety!" One would think that in such a percolating metropolis, famous for its culture and learning, that connecting with other people would be a highly prized and promoted value.

Alas, exchanging eye contact while toddling along the sidewalks of the city was *verboten*, and was seen as a sure invitation to trouble. Yet, in such a menagerie of humanity, one couldn't help but stare. There was so much to take in amidst this vast sea of people and creative human energy.

Flannery O'Connor, the great American Catholic novelist, in a piece addressed to writers, says something applicable to all of us: "The writer should never be ashamed of staring. There is nothing that doesn't require his attention." O'Connor's advice to writers, that they keep their eyes and hearts open to the world around them, even if that means, at times, *fixating* for extended periods of time, is worthy advice for everyone, especially followers of Christ, who are sons and daughters of the Creator of the Universe.

Contemplation, a major practice of the spiritual life, has at its heart, fixing one's attention on created gifts of God, so to be drawn up into paying a deeper attention to the Creator. Contemplation, appreciation, gratitude, and thanksgiving for God's creation—whether human or otherwise—begins by staring, by focusing

"'Despite What Our Mothers May Have Taught Us, It Is Good To Stare"

deeply and penetratingly upon what God has wrought. If we spend most of our life turning away from what fascinates us, or worse yet, simply skimming over the top of creation like dragonflies skittering above the water, we will never reach the depth of soulful living to which God invites us. What truly seems then to be "impolite" is ignoring the multiple opportunities we are given each day to stop, to stare, and to relish the beauty that God is creating as God splashes God's brush against the canvas of our world.

One of the great gifts that creative people bring to us, whether in poetry, prose, music, paint, marble, or in a host of other ways, is the gift of freezing us in our normally distracted and discombobulated meanderings, and allowing us to pay attention, to focus, to center in on someone or something of beauty or challenge. Artists take the time to stop and stare at what life offers up, whether it be energizing or debilitating, and then set out to lure us, the unobservant ones, into what they see. They set out to lure us into contemplation.

I had such an occasion to be visually lured into contemplation when I traveled to Santa Fe, New Mexico and visited the Georgia O'Keeffe Museum. American icon Georgia O'Keeffe, who inhabited the desert outside Taos, New Mexico at her Ghost Ranch compound, had no trouble inviting people to stare. In fact, she helped us along the way by her extraordinary, indeed revolutionary artistic approach to flower painting. If you are not familiar with O'Keeffe, her work is populated by canvas after canvas of enlarged, magnificently colored blossoms—blossoms on steroids, if you will—that cannot help but be stared upon.

At one point in her life, someone asked O'Keeffe why she painted flowers in such a gargantuan format. Here's how she responded:

I decided that if I could paint that flower in a huge scale, you could not ignore its beauty. When you see a flower…and really look at it, it's your world for the moment. I want to give that world to someone else. Most people in the city rush around so, they have no time to look at a flower. I want them to see it whether they want to or not. Nobody sees a flower, really; it is so small. We haven't time, and to see it takes time—like a friend takes time.

Many people never seem to reach a satisfying connection in their relationship with God, Jesus and the Church, the living presence of Christ drawn together in the Holy Spirit—a real depth in their spiritual life—because there's no time for **staring**, for truly *observing* the work of the Spirit within and around them. No wonder we use the phrase, "to **pay** attention"—because staring, observing, connecting, and being aware all ***cost*** us considerably. There is a price we pay for living with depth to our lives.

Despite what our parents and teachers have preached since an early age, perhaps one of the cardinal rules of the spiritual life should be: STOP AND STARE AS OFTEN AS POSSIBLE—GOD FINDS IT IMPOLITE IF WE DON'T!

While I take many things my mother has said to heart and have woven them into the fabric of my life over the years (and to be honest, as she would surely admit, there are plenty of things I have disregarded or conveniently forgotten), there is one bit of motherly wisdom worth turning on its head: ***Despite what our mothers may have taught us, it is good to stare!"***

Life Lesson:

"It's Much Easier To See Through A Window Than A Door"

"It's Much Easier To See Through A Window Than A Door"

Eucharistic adoration has been making a methodical comeback in Catholic life. Not that we have forgotten it completely, but the time the average Catholic spent in front of the Blessed Sacrament, reserved in the tabernacle of a church, had declined steadily over the past decades. There are many suppositions as to why this is the case, and the "answers" to this development are far more complex than most people who make a deliberate stand in either advocating more devotion to the reserved presence of Christ, or those who dismiss it as "so Middle Ages" are willing to admit. Much as the media uses sound bytes to convey as little information as possible to the masses, so go the banner-like arguments voiced by both supporters and detractors of Eucharistic adoration.

Surely, spending sacred time in meditation and reflection, humbly placing oneself before the Body of Christ reserved in the tabernacle, needs no justification. It is an extension of the Eucharist we celebrate, consume, and share in the sacrifice of the Mass. But there are surely cautions as well, especially when one's Eucharistic adoration goes no further than the door of the tabernacle. *It is much easier to see through a window than a door.*

One of my favorite sacred spaces can be found at the

"It's Much Easier To See Through A Window Than A Door"

Eucharistic chapel of the Norbertine community of Santa Maria de la Vid in Albuquerque, New Mexico, where I have spent time on personal retreats. Set on the western mesa just beyond the city, the Norbertine retreat combines the beauty and silence of the desert, with sweeping, grand views of the mountain ranges that surround Albuquerque. As one enters the adobe pueblo-like structure that is the priory church, although surrounded by all the modern amenities of contemporary worship spaces, there is an overwhelming sense that one is stepping back in time.

This sacramental surge is conjured not only by the design of the space, but by the "ancient ones" whose presence is immediately felt within the walls of the church. These "ancient ones" are both Catholic and Native. As the community of faith gathers for Eucharistic liturgies, as well as Liturgy of the Hours, supplicants are surrounded both by life-size statues of Catholic saints (who incidentally sit on the same level as the worshippers, signifying that they are praying with us every time we gather in liturgy), and by the intangible, but no less palpable presence of the "first peoples," who seem to rise out of the sacred mesa dirt upon which the church sits, once home to the Anasazi peoples.

Leaving the main, circular worship space and walking a few short steps through a passageway, one enters the Eucharistic chapel in all its profound simplicity. It is impossible to sit in this space and gaze upon the reserved Blessed Sacrament without seeing what lives beyond the door to the tabernacle. A massive, clear-paned, floor-to-ceiling window graces the eastern wall of the chapel. There is no way to fix one's eyes upon the tabernacle, the reserved Body of Christ, and not be drawn into the world that moves and groans just beyond those tiny, carved wooden doors.

To adore the Body of Christ in the tabernacle must always

lead one to adore the Body of Christ as it lives and breathes in the world God has created. After all, the Body of Christ is just that—a "body"—flesh and blood and marrow, emotions and wants and needs, hurts and joys and disappointments, confusions and certainties and wonder. To adore the Body of Christ is to keep one's gaze firmly fixed on the world where the Body and Blood of Christ is broken and shared countless more times than on any altar in any church.

Pope John Paul II, in his Apostolic Letter opening the *Year of the Eucharist* in 2004, while speaking to the promotion and power of Eucharistic adoration before the door of the tabernacle, emphasized throughout his message the radical importance of seeing out through our church windows into a world in radical need of Eucharistic presence. He called upon followers of Christ:

> *…to commit themselves in a particular way to responding with fraternal solicitude to one of the many forms of poverty present in our world. I think for example of the tragedy of hunger which plagues hundreds of millions of human beings, the diseases which afflict developing countries, the loneliness of the elderly, the hardships faced by the unemployed, the struggles of immigrants. These are evils which are present—albeit to a different degree—even in areas of immense wealth. We cannot delude ourselves: by our mutual love and, in particular, by our concern for those in need we will be recognized as true followers of Christ (cf. John 13:35; Matthew 25:31-46). This will be the criterion by which the authenticity of our Eucharistic celebrations is judged* (Mane Nobiscum Domine, no. 28).

"It's Much Easier To See Through A Window Than A Door"

To adore the Body of Christ in the tabernacle must always lead to a seeing beyond the doors of that sacred receptacle, for Christ cannot be held prisoner, whether for worship or adoration, but must instead be freed to make his home in all creation, especially in the broken and wounded humanity, whose stripes he continues to bear, whose blood still cries out from the crosses to which humankind is nailed every day.

The great St. John Chrysostom once profoundly challenged his listeners in a homily in this way:

Do you wish to honor the body of Christ? Do not ignore him when he is naked. Do not pay him homage in the temple clad in silk, only then to neglect him outside where he is cold and ill-clad. He who said: 'This is my body' is the same who said: 'You saw me hungry and you gave me no food', and 'Whatever you did to the least of my brothers you did also to me'... What good is it if the Eucharistic table is overloaded with golden chalices when your brother is dying of hunger? Start by satisfying his hunger and then with what is left you may adorn the altar as well (In Evangelium S. Matthaei, Homily 50).

The famous artist Henri Matisse, conversing with his lifelong friend, Sr. Jacques-Marie regarding what he considered his greatest masterpiece, "The Chapel of the Rosary" in Vence, France, responded to her curious query. Sr. Jacques-Marie noticed that from inside the chapel, one could see the outside world through the windows, perhaps determining that this might be some troublesome distraction to those who came to the chapel for prayer and worship. Matisse simply said, "Of course, you have to pray for them too."

While one can speak of "private" time in prayer before the Blessed Sacrament, in truth there can be nothing "private" about conversing with the Lord Jesus, for to approach his heart and divinity, is to find there the whole of humanity and the created order.

I think the Norbertines got it right in Albuquerque; they provided a window to the world in close proximity to the doorway to the tabernacle. And isn't this precisely what "communion" is all about? Being joined to Christ and his sacred Body means to feed the hungers and thirsts of the world, just as he did at the Last Supper and continues to do at every supper where we gather in his name.

May we begin to make the time to pray before the Blessed Sacrament in our church, and let our adoration of Christ's living presence in the reserved sacrament always find us *looking beyond the door.*

After all, the lesson clearly is: **It's much easier to see through a window than a door."**

Life Lesson:

"IN ORDER TO SOAR WITH THE SPIRIT, YOU MUST FIRST GET TO THE BOTTOM"

"In Order To Soar With The Spirit, You Must First Get To The Bottom"

Usually, I get a late start on Lent; at least that seems to have been the case as I look back on the past several years. I suppose, from my days as a pastor and now as a Lenten mission revival preacher, I spend more time prior to Ash Wednesday worrying about getting everyone else ready for Lent—lining up liturgies, reviewing Christian Initiation rituals, dividing up the ashes, pressing the purple clothes, deciding on adult prayer and enrichment, re-locating the rules on fast and abstinence, developing new words of inspiration to fire the imagination of revival attendees for conversion—that before I know it, it's week number three of Lent, and I'm just getting focused on *my* spirituality!

Well, one particular year, I vowed that things would be different! In addition to focusing on the ministry to others, I gave myself the leisure to think about *my Lent*, and where I might be going. And I decided—after much thought, reading, and prayer—I was digging in! That year, like Jesus facing his Jerusalem, I decided to firmly set my face to **GOING UNDERGROUND!**

I intended to "go underground" in the sense of seeking more spiritual depth, delving further below my surface spirituality and routine activities, entering through the dark and hidden (and

"In Order To Soar With The Spirit, You Must First Get To The Bottom"

troubling) caverns of my spirit. Somehow, I was coming to the insight that ***in order to soar with the Spirit, I first had to get to the bottom.***

While we still tend to imagine Lent to be the time for "giving up" or "adding on" for a few weeks—it is still the season that belongs most especially to the Catechumens—those preparing for Initiation into the Church. And so, those of us already baptized into Christ take our lead from them—and we pursue our self-and-community examinations because we too need recommitment to the waters of new life we have already received. To be baptized into Christ Jesus is to *go down with him*—so that we may one day rise with him to the fullness of God's life!

I figured, if this is good enough theology and spirituality and liturgical practice for the Elect, it was good enough for me (who feels like my "election" came in another millennium)!

Although Jesus admonishes us through Matthew's Ash Wednesday Gospel to do our praying and fasting "in secret," rather than make a show of our Lenten efforts, in that particular Lenten season, my guiding cue and lesson did not emanate from those challenging words. Instead, I was moved by another image, a more recent spiritual experience.

The previous summer, while on retreat in New Mexico, I had the good fortune of entering into two sacred spaces occupied centuries ago by Native Americans. These sacred spaces are known as **kivas**, which is the Hopi word for *ceremonial room*. While there is some scholarly debate about the full nature of these underground chambers, it is widely accepted that the kivas were the center of spiritual activity for the community (sorry, *men only*, though).

While on pilgrimage one day near the end of my retreat, I visited an amazing round, subterranean chamber once occupied by the Anasazi peoples, entering into it by descending a ladder poking out of a singular opening in the roof. With replicas of murals painted on the walls, a reconstruction of the Native American spiritual art that once graced the circular dirt walls, I felt as though I had entered a different world, a different plane of existence. In the center of the kiva, there was a hole in the floor, called a *sipapu* [SEE-pah-puh/Hopi], which symbolized the navel of the earth from which the ancient ancestors were said to have emerged when they entered the present world. Thus, the symbolic connection between the people and Mother Earth was given tangible form.

I keep a small replica of a kiva ladder in my office, and while meditating one day about the path my Lenten journey might take, catching sight of the ladder, now draped with a century old Navajo birthing blanket, I was brought back in spirit to my August journey into the ancient kivas of the Pueblo and Anasazi peoples—and in doing so—I found my path—and the challenge, not only for that particular Lenten journey, but in fact, a challenge, a lesson for every journey in life: **In order to soar with the Spirit, you must first get to the bottom**. In other words, it's important to go underground, to get beneath the surface before floating in the clouds.

Many ancient peoples have always looked deep into and beneath the earth for images of meaningful spirituality. Our own Christian faith shares this same exploration, as we celebrate the Son of God, Jesus the Christ, who had to "go underground" before being raised on high by the Father. In Jesus' words, "unless a grain of wheat falls to the ground and is buried, it remains just a grain of wheat." Before Jesus could be "lifted up" so as to draw all creation to himself, he first had to get to the bottom of his very self, shedding the last drop of his precious blood.

"In Order To Soar With The Spirit, You Must First Get To The Bottom"

In a similar vein, St. Paul starkly unnerves us with his powerful question: "Do you not realize that you were baptized into Christ's death?" Yes, to recover our souls, we too must go underground, beneath the many veneers and protective surfaces with which we hide our true selves, and meet our selves, and the God who dwells in the depths, face-to-face.

The great American mystical poet and spiritual seeker, Ralph Waldo Emerson, as Thomas Moore reminds us, said that *he couldn't have the 'elevation' [of spirit] that he wanted because he didn't have sufficient bottom (cf. The Soul's Religion).* In other words, Emerson knew that to "soar with the Spirit," we must first "get to the bottom," to go underground, to visit the depths of who we are.

But, as we know all too well, and why, even as I first wrote these words many years ago, still safely distant from Ash Wednesday, hesitant about my pending path—journeys to the depths, our depths, are frightening. The dark, hidden, mysterious regions of our souls are fraught with memories and disappointments and losses we may shudder to encounter or revisit. There are "crypts" within each of us where we think we have laid to rest old wounds, lost loves, shattered dreams, sinful choices—and we want to stay clear of those cemeteries, lest what we thought was dead and gone isn't really so, and now may come back to trouble us once again.

I recall how tentatively I descended the rickety rungs of the kiva ladder on the sacred grounds near the Rio Grande River in Albuquerque, unaware of what I might find when I hit bottom, unprepared for the mysterious etchings on the walls I was about to encounter—the pictured-stories of past triumphs and defeats. And now, as the rungs of my ladder were about to be placed through the opening of yet another sacred Lenten season on Ash Wednesday, I knew that once again my steps would be tentative, that the descent below the surface features of my life would be slow. But I prayed that the strength of the Holy Spirit, who lives in the deepest part of who God has created me to be and to become, would allow me to enter that sacred space, to visit the depths, so that on Easter morning, I could truly know what it means to *rise with Christ.*

May you find the courage to willingly risk the journey "underground." For I surely believe that **in order to soar with the Spirit, you must first get to the bottom.**

Life Lesson:

"When Face To Face With Mystery, It's Best Not To Grab It"

"When Face To Face With Mystery, It's Best Not To Grab It"

Generally speaking, I find little value on television, so I don't spend a lot of time in front of it. I suppose that I am part of that tiny percentage of Americans that advertisers and trendsetters ignore, since I don't get enough exposure to their assaults for my money. I do, however, enjoy the occasional specials on the History Channel, or Discovery, or PBS, or perhaps an intriguing segment of "Unsolved Mysteries."

Last summer, I spent a week in Santa Fe, New Mexico. It was my first time there, and I didn't leave many stones unturned in that town. I believe my tired feet crossed the threshold of nearly every art gallery that I could locate. The beauty of all my hoofing around old Santa Fe is that I was able to indulge in all the fine cuisine there without gaining a pound!

Amongst the many beautiful people and things I experienced in Santa Fe, one stands above the others: the Loretto Chapel and its magnificent, mysterious and "miraculous" staircase. In case you aren't familiar with the legend of the spiral staircase, allow me to quickly summarize the tale.

After the Chapel had been built, there was no access to the small choir loft located 22' above the chapel floor. (I suppose, like many church building projects today, finances dictated that

"When Face To Face With Mystery, It's Best Not To Grab It"

parts of the project had to be left behind—thus a choir loft with no way to get up to it!). When the Sisters of the chapel eventually decided to have a staircase built to the loft, carpenters told them that because of architectural limitations, no such stairway could ever be constructed, and that only a ladder could be used to access the choir loft. The legend says that the Sisters began a Novena to St. Joseph, patron of carpenters, and on the ninth day of the novena, a man riding a donkey and carrying a toolbox appeared at the chapel looking for work. After a couple of months, when the staircase was finished, the man vanished, unable to be located, even though the Sisters posted ads in the local newspapers. The Sisters ultimately believed that indeed it was St. Joseph himself who had come to their tiny chapel in Santa Fe and completed the work. What the man left behind, whoever he was, is the mysterious and miraculous Loretto Chapel Staircase.

The staircase is revered not only because of the mysterious carpenter, but also because of the sheer physics of its design and construction. The staircase makes two 360° turns with no visible signs of support, and there are no identifiable nails in the structure, only wooden pegs!

It is quite a beautiful sight—but the problem, and the source of my particular frustration on the day I basked in its mysterious glory, is that I couldn't get close enough to it to touch it! The roping that marked off the bottom of the staircase was set at just the right distance so that it was beyond anyone's reach. The beauty and magic and mystery of this holy icon were drawing me (and apparently everyone else in the chapel that day) like a magnet to want to get at least a finger on it—but under the watchful gaze of the security people, there wasn't a chance.

And don't think I didn't try! I lingered long enough, hoping that at the moment one of the security or guides turned their heads toward another part of the chapel, I would spring into action and then run out the door. After waiting what seemed like forever for the opportunity that never came, I departed, coming to the realization—not only about the Miraculous Spiral Staircase of the Loretto Chapel, but with all that we label "Mystery"—**that the best thing we can do in the presence and face of mystery is to simply "approach" it—not lay hold of it completely.**

The life lesson that slowly began to touch my heart was this: ***When face to face with Mystery, it's best not to grab it!"***

Several weeks after returning from this pilgrimage of sorts, I celebrated the great Feast of Pentecost, followed by the Solemnity of the Most Holy Trinity, and then again a week after that, the Solemnity of the Most Holy Body and Blood of Christ—three of the most profound mysteries of the Catholic faith. And yet, as central as they are to Catholic life, how can we comprehend their meaning? How can we grasp hold of the immensity of the Spirit and her multitudinous gifts, the intimate relationship of three persons in one God, or the incredible gift of Christ's total sacrifice of self for our eternal well-being and union with God? How can we begin to understand a God who is so far beyond us, yet sustains every breath we take? How can we touch the mystery of the God who daily touches us in oh so subtle and marvelous ways?

Like the awesomely beautiful Miraculous Spiral Staircase of Loretto Chapel, perhaps the best we can do, the only thing we can do, is ***approach***—to see *some* of the beauty, to touch a *piece* of the wonder, to feel a *brush* of the warmth, to comprehend a *paragraph* of the great story.

It seems that it is in our human nature to want more than simply to "approach." In fact, we are often led to believe that we

"When Face To Face With Mystery, It's Best Not To Grab It"

are to grab and clutch and lay hold, by whatever means possible, to what we want or believe we deserve or are "owed" by others. But God works differently; God works within the cloud of mystery—and mystery is never meant to be "solved"; rather it is meant to be *approached*, to be *savored*—tenderly, gingerly, with reverence and awe—and with deep appreciation and love for the God who showers us with goodness and blessing.

Not unlike my ill-fated attempts to touch the holy staircase in Santa Fe, I am sure that at times in my life, I will continue to want to do more than approach the mystery of God and the baffling mysteries of the life God sets before me. Yes, I will continue to want to grab more than I can handle or that I need to know. I will demand explanations and satisfactory answers to deep questions. And yes, while still allowing me to make my blind stabs and attempts, God will continue to remind me in subtle or perhaps more aggressive ways (whichever God believes I need at the moment) that savoring a tiny taste, breathing a wisp of fragrance, putting a tip of my finger into a magnificent stream, or simply catching a heart-warming sight out of the corner of my eye can be more satisfying, more exhilarating, more holy than having it all.

Poetic Interlude

"On Gazing Out the Chapel Window"

Norbertine Community Church, Santa Maria de la Vid
Albuquerque, New Mexico

On this side of the window's panes…I sit.
Framed, calming and centering.
On that side of the window's panes…it sits.
World, spreading out under the haze and windswept earth.
Framed, too, by jagged sacred mountains of Native faith.
World, forced out centrifugally, by unending tumult of
      striving, borrowing, spending, yearning, wandering.
Not all calming or centering, but swirling—
      an occasional gust of hope ratcheting up the sound.

And between us, standing sentinel, the Body and Blood,
Framed, too, by a box, carved and polished and gilded, but yearning
to be swept up and out
through the frame and into the distance,
      where food and drink need multiplied again for the
      thousands, arranged now, not in
      beds of daisies and lilies of the field, but
      in plots of concrete, adobe, and dusty, parched despair.

On this side of the window's panes...I sit
    wondering, as the lilting hawk glides by,
    held up by grace and freedom,
    who will dismantle these frames and let
    the in out and the out in.
And a voice echoes, through the window's panes
(and pains),
    bounced from a marble, seven-stepped sanctuary
    set amidst pasture and the heart that summer's
    day after its (my) birth, and
    through twenty-two years of cavernous miles and
    God knows what—
"Here I am Lord, send me!"

Benjamin Berinti
May 1, 2007

    I wrote this poem while sitting in the Priory's Eucharistic chapel and gazing out its beautiful, large picture window. The chapel speaks to me of the Eucharist as a window on the world, not meant to remain "boxed" and "framed" in this simple, yet beautiful chapel—but rather to move out into the world and all its cares that rest just beyond my gaze in this moment. And I, in my priesthood, am sent to carry it forth.

Life Lesson:

"Every Pearl Always Starts As A Pain-In-The-Shell"

"Every Pearl Always Starts as a Pain-in-the-Shell"

Despite the fact that I am currently engaging the wonders of modern technology in order to make this book available to readers, I am by no means a child of technology. In truth, I usually describe myself as a technological dinosaur—and I handle the gizmos and gadgets of the tech world like a T-Rex trying to peel a hard-boiled egg!

I admit it…I simply love paper! I like writing on it, reading from it, crumpling it when the words are not coming out the way I desire, tearing it to pieces when I'm really frustrated, lining shelf after shelf with it in my library, wrapping presents with it, and getting the ink from it on my fingers and under my nails while I spend a whole week leisurely paging through my Sunday *New York Times*.

No wonder then, while perusing a book store for a new volume to take with me on my upcoming retreat to a little cabin north of Albuquerque, near the tiny speck of a town called Jemez Springs, the following title seemingly leapt from the shelf right into my hands: Julia Cameron's *The Sound of Paper*.

I seem to have good fortune this way. Perhaps the Holy Spirit likes to help me jump start my time in the prayer and communion with God that I desire while on retreat. Whenever I'm seeking a book that might give me inspiration, but I haven't a clue to a specific title or author, as I simply scan the shelves of the "religion and spirituality" section, somehow the perfect book's title spine lights up for me like a billboard on the Las Vegas strip…and I eventually reap the insights and wisdom of its pages throughout my retreat. It has been a rare occasion that I've been disappointed.

While perched on the wraparound porch of the circular cottage I inhabited at the Redondo Retreat Center, nestled just beyond the border of the quirky town of Jemez Springs, New Mexico, tucked high along a mountain ridge, I was thoroughly enjoying Cameron's work. I had read several of her books before, but this collection of essays was particularly moving and seemed to be touching me just where I need to be comforted, cajoled, and careened in a new direction.

One particular reflection Julia Cameron opened for me has lead to this life lesson: **Every pearl always starts as a pain-in-the-shell!** Allow me to share the gist of her reflection mingled with what I have since discovered.

Pearls, those lovely, expensive, and oh-so-proud-to-be-worn symbols of love and affection are born when an oyster or some other type of mollusk is irritated by the invasion of something disturbing, something that doesn't belong, and something that is breaking into the oyster's comfy, cozy, sealed environment. After all, that's the beauty of having a shell, isn't it? You can always close the hatch whenever you don't want to be bothered; and you can set the time and place when the shell is to be opened again.

Some speck of sand or microscopic shrimp wanders into the unsuspecting oyster's soft, slimy lair—and gets stuck there. Once the oyster recognizes there's an intruder in the premises, the oyster begins a furious attempt to expel the intruder, to ease

"Every Pearl Always Starts As A Pain-In-The-Shell"

the discomfort, to rid itself of the unwanted interloper. But the harder the oyster tries to rid itself of the nemesis, the force of its churning and grinding ends up not expelling the intruder, but rather results in the slow formation of what eventually becomes a pearl!

Consequently, in truth, a pearl is nothing more than a disturbance; something that isn't supposed to be there. And this "something that isn't supposed to be there" needs to be attended to, done away with, gotten rid of.

During a reflection day for parish ministers to the sick, I was sharing this very lesson about the pearl, when one of the participants, who hailed from a Caribbean island nation, took me aside and said: "We have a word for 'pearl' in our native language; a word that literally means a pearl is the ***'tears of the oyster'***." What a wonderful metaphor that captures the truth of this life lesson.

How often in the course of the days of our lives do we encounter interruptions, intrusions, disruptions, and things that we deem "don't belong"? How often do we find something we neither desire nor feel prepared for entering into, even sneaking into our well-laid plans and programs?

This life lesson invites me to revisit my notions of interruptions, forces me to reexamine what constitutes an intrusion into my own plans and purposes. I'm not sure that after this reexamination I am always clear about how to make distinctions between pure interruptions or a repeated lack of committed self-care and nurturing and those meaningful intrusions that result in unexpected, unplanned, and uninvited God-moments. These distinctions are made even more difficult to discern since it appears that the God of Christian revelation is notoriously experienced as *interruptive*!

The Scriptures are littered with descriptions of a God who disrupts the plans of human beings, redirects their courses of action, makes them move from one place to another in search of a promised land, uses parabolic methods of teaching that couch deep truths in simple, disarming stories, blurs the lines of who is in and who is out when it comes to religious boundaries, reverses relationships of power and control, fills the poor and empties the rich, announces that *metanoia,* a radical about-face is at the heart of discipleship, and demonstrates that one must pass from death to life. The track record of the God of Abraham, Isaac, Jacob, Sarah, Miriam, Moses, Ruth, Esther, Jeremiah, and Jesus is long and wide with interrupting human ways and means. In the clearest fashion of all, the "Great Interrupter" announces in the scriptures that ultimately, *my ways are not your ways!* How's that for mincing no words about who it is that sets the agenda?

We are not alone in our experience of interruptions, of things we deem irritating—the Gospels clearly show us Jesus and his disciples battling similar intrusions. Mark 4:35-41 relates the story of Jesus calming the storm, but only after his much-deserved nap time is interrupted by a somewhat comically frightened band of apostles.

I'm always amused by this particular story of the apostles. The majority of them were fisherman, right? And one would think they had seen more than their fair share of terrifying storms in the course of making their living. And so here they are now, running around like kindergartners being chased by the Cookie Monster…and they come crying to the Lord to save them. But this intrusion, this irritation ultimately gives birth to an experience of Jesus as the powerful Christ of God, and the pearl of a declaration of faith made possible only because of this disruption.

"Every Pearl Always Starts As A Pain-In-The-Shell"

Mark 5:25-34 finds Jesus spinning around in a large crowd of people, who are being squeezed together like sardines in a tin can, and demanding to know "who touched me?" The disciples, seeming more sensible than their usual portrayal in the scriptures, simply try to calm down the Lord and gingerly suggest that it might be easier to find a specific grain of sand in the desert than to determine the identity of the misguided grabber! But in the end, this disturbance, this intrusion into Jesus' life results in the pearl-like beauty of a much-needed miracle for a woman who wanted nothing more than to feel the hem of his garment. She didn't even want a face-to-face meeting, just a little thread to hold on to.

Another humorous account of irritating disturbance is related in Mark 6:30-33. Here Jesus and his apostles head off to the other side of the lake, to what they assumed would be an "out of the way place," for some rest, rejuvenation and communion with the Father. But lo and behold, even before they reach the shores of their hideaway, the crowds have already arrived ahead of them! I chuckle when I think that the quickest way from Point A to Point B is supposed to be a straight line, and that was the movement of Jesus and the apostles. Somehow, however, those who took the longer route made it there first. But in the end, this disturbance, too, will result in a miraculous feeding of a multitude. The pearls of numerous fish and loaves of bread are strewn among thousands. Something beautiful again is borne from the throes of intrusion and disruption.

And this lesson comes to life in my own experiences, as surely it does in yours.

Over the course of time that I served as the pastor of two different parishes, 3:00 AM calls to the hospital were not uncommon.

I have to admit that each time the phone would rouse me from sleep, and knowing that it most likely was a clarion call to head to one of the hospitals or nursing homes in Orlando, most likely to be with someone near death, I did not automatically leap from my bed with a burning joy in my heart to have yet another opportunity to minister God's grace and comfort! No, in my dull-headed sleepiness, I wanted to stay in bed, and more than that, there was definitely something less than a prayer on my lips as I struggled to make myself somewhat presentable for going out and being seen in public at that time of the morning! And it never seemed to fail that these intruding calls came either after a tremendously long and strenuous day, or right before what would be an earlier than normal wake-up call for a strenuous and lengthy day to come!

Yet each time this disturbance and interruption occurred, on my drive home from the hospital, I knew why I had been called and what "pearl" had been formed in that crucible of life. Sometimes, the pearl didn't even come from the specific person to whose bedside I was summoned. At times, the pearl was formed by talking with an attending nurse, or meeting someone coming up with me on the elevator, or perhaps even from being unexpectedly invited into a patient's room other than the one to which I had been called.

Every once in awhile, someone will stop me after a Sunday morning liturgy, or grab me in the middle of wolfing down a ham sandwich at a church luncheon, or stop me midway between the pickles and rice in the grocery store aisle, and utter these infamous words, "Do you have a minute, Fr. Ben?"

Although at that moment I have no idea what may be on the mind of the person making the inquiry, this much I do know

"Every Pearl Always Starts As A Pain-In-The-Shell"

without a doubt—whatever it is…it's going to take far more than a minute! In fact, I liken these conversations to that of the mathematics surrounding the age of a dog. For every minute the person tells me it will take to address their concerns or issues, I simply multiply that by seven…and even then it usually doesn't come close to how much time this little interruption will take.

But once again, so many times, something beautiful has been borne from these unexpected, often unwanted, and usually unfocused conversations. They become provocations, catalysts for pearls of great price.

While vacationing in Hull, Massachusetts one fine summer, I happened to take a long trek from the Benedictine abbey where I was staying all the way to Nantasket Beach. I stayed the course on my way to the beach, following the twists and turns of the road exactly the way I had been instructed to by one of the resident monks. However, on the return trip, someone I got off course and came face-to-face with a large, uninviting sign that read: "WRONG WAY!" Well, feeling a little more adventurous than normal (after all, I was relaxing on vacation), I disregarded the sign, intruded on the path of the "wrong way," and ended up traveling a colorful route that eventually led to one of the most magnificent views of the ocean I had witnessed to that point in my stay in Hull. I was intoxicated by the beauty and majesty of the surrounding cliffs, the multi-colored ocean waters, the billowy clouds overhead, the Clorox-clean sails of the passing boats—and it all came to me only because I intruded on the "wrong way," got lost and wandered into a place I wasn't supposed to be.

At times, as I've discovered in these and many other experiences, once I put aside my own frustrations over inconvenience and twisted time tables, once I rearrange priorities and agenda, once I forgive my own unfaithfulness to projects and plans that I deem paramount, once I wrestle with trying to find a balance between my own needs and the always pressing needs of others—it is then, with God's grace, I am able to live into this life lesson, to find that often, at the heart of some interruption, rests the antidote I need for a weary soul, the insight required to make a decision, the reorientation toward the commitment and values I am seeking. At the heart of many an irritating intrusion is the face of God yearning to be seen, the voice of God crying to be heard, the pain of God aching to be attended to, the nourishment of God waiting to be consumed, and the love of God eager to be wrapped around me.

Every pearl always starts as a pain-in-the-shell. Julia Cameron's prompting in her wonderful book, and my further reflection upon and consequent living into this life lesson simply interjects a major "CAUTION!" into the things I first deem to be intrusions, interruptions, disturbances, or things I quickly judge to "not belong here."

Make no mistake about it, though, there is no 20-20 clarity of vision in discerning whether it is the finger of God agitating below the surface of my own designs and needs, or simply someone else's selfish hand tugging at the fringes of my heart for attention that would best be met with a firmer, stronger rebuke, or the courage and wisdom on my part to simply say *no*! A lack of proper self care, ignoring signs of burnout and despair, looking away from much needed personal time and nurturing, always giving but making little room for receiving, trying to constantly rescue rather than let be—all these conspire to bring great harm to us, and ultimately, minimal help to others. Our wells, from which we and others drink so frequently, especially as we strive

"Every Pearl Always Starts As A Pain-In-The-Shell"

to be a giving, generous people, are not bottomless. There is only one source from which endless water flows, welling up to eternal life. The only source from which we can drink abundantly and never fear the onset of the last drop is Jesus Christ! As for us our wells can and do run dry.

And when our wells teeter on the edge of giving up their last ounce of refreshment, when they become dry and dusty, God does replenish. Yet, the life lesson that ***every pearl always starts as a pain-in-the-shell*** is that the replenishment that God sends our way, the rains of regeneration and renewal that God graciously showers upon the parched, weary, brittle contours of our lives does not always come according to our plans and designs. In fact, often those very plans and designs are interrupted by God.

Mysteriously woven into the fabric of distractions and irritations, of disturbances and interruptions of well-laid, well-deserved plans are threads of insight, wisdom, strength, clearer vision, health and wholeness. In the middle of sick children, unplanned pregnancies, ill health, fender-benders, job losses, missed airplanes, financial shortfalls, unsolicited phone calls or door knocks, incessant pleas for attention from wounded spouses or friends, miscalculated time commitments, bad news, and a whole host of other *pains-in-the-shell*, rests a mysterious God who often makes use of such experiences for helping us grow in wisdom and grace. Sometimes, while we are busy, as author Martha Manning calls it *chasing grace*, grace in fact comes to us.

What our life lesson calls for in a practical way is to pause and linger over the meaning of some interruption, to wrestle with its untimely intrusion, rather than make quick work of the distraction and return to our original plan or project. When we allow ourselves and our plans to be penetrated more deeply by people and experiences which seem, on first blush, to merely be disruptions, when we allow ourselves the luxury of reflection upon the dynamics of the particular encounter or task that presents itself to us, when we wrestle with rather than quickly begrudge the presence of this interruption in our lives, it is then that we may be privileged with a God-moment, a God-encounter that accomplishes the very replenishment we have been seeking.

Be alert, be cautious then. The next disturbance or irritation *may* just be a provocation, a catalyst, a pearl of great price forming. Like the *tears of the oyster*, the *tears* that are flowing from some experience, encounter, or relationship in our life at this moment, *may* just be what is bringing something beautiful to life, a prelude or perhaps part of the process of creating some blessing, grace, gift, healing, or new opening. God is so often lurking somewhere around the edges of our plans and designs, waiting to break through our defenses in the guise of an interruption, some *pain-in-our-shell*.

Life Lesson:

"SOMETIMES YOU GET TO THE DOOR, BUT YOU CAN'T GO THROUGH"

"Sometimes You Get To The Door, But You Can't Go Through"

Sitting high above the sleepy town of Jemez Springs, lodged amidst the red rocks of the jagged landscape, I spent most of my retreat days wandering the hills and trails surrounding my roundhouse cabin. Hiking always takes me back to a childhood filled with whole day treks through the woods that framed my boyhood homes. I loved the woods, and so did my brother and our friends. Hiking, trail-blazing, hanging rope swings from huge limbs and careening over gorges, looking for frogs and little lobsters in the creeks (*pronounced 'cricks' in Pittsburghese*), erecting forts and tree houses—all were part of leisurely weekends and long summer vacation days.

On one particular jaunt for the day, two experiences first prompted, and upon further reflection, coalesced into this life lesson: ***Sometimes you get to the door, but you can't go through.***

I spied some magnificent cliff rocks in the distance, and as I walked, I hoped to get the best angle on their beauty in order to take some photographs. Now my photography skills are extremely limited, and I recognize that no photo you ever take on a vacation or adventure *ever* captures what your eyes are beholding. That's why I'm a firm believer in postcards! Despite this knowledge, I insisted to myself that I would get as close as I could to the

"Sometimes You Get To The Door, But You Can't Go Through"

base of these tent rock cliffs as I could, and I'd just start snapping away, praying that at least one snap would result in immortalizing what my gaze was feasting upon.

But here's the problem…the more I walked in the direction of the cliffs, the farther away they seemed to become! No matter which path, which trail, which angle I took as a detour in pursuit of the perfect photo, I seemed to be getting no closer to the tent rocks. Half frustrated and half amused at my dilemma, I couldn't understand the logistics of this adventure. I knew I hadn't been in the hills so long that I was beginning to hallucinate from lack of water, nor did I assume the mountains and hills were leaping for joy (as the scriptures say)—away from my sight. In the end, there were a few feeble attempts at photos, but none came remotely close to the beauty, power, majesty and play-of-sun upon those gleaming tent rocks. ***Sometimes you get to the door, but you can't go through.***

While making the ill-fated journey I have just described, I noticed a wonderful rock jutting out from the side of a hill, and it struck me that this would be a magnificent perch from which to gaze out into the valley and to be thoroughly inspired with words for my journal. As I looked up from underneath its reaching ledge, a vision from my *Golden Books Children's Bible* came to me—there was Moses, perched on a ledge not unlike the one I now stood beneath, as he was staring out into the Promised Land, his stiff-necked people milling about beneath him, ready to seize their land of milk and honey after so many decades of sojourning. In that moment, my need to climb the hill and reach that sacred perch was sealed, and I planned to do just that the following day.

With the frustrations of my search for a dynamic angle on the tent rocks a day behind me, I was all the more determined to return to the path that would take me to the rock ledge, for what

I believed was to become the place of my own *burning bush*, and where I might finally begin to write the book that everyone had been telling me for years to write. Once finding the spot along the trail, I was confident that today's results would outpace yesterday's disaster, as I could clearly see a trail winding along the base of the ledge, heading like a snake's tail right to the top, and the place of my expectant joy.

"Snake's tail," now there's the hitch! As I was focused upon the climbing task at hand, refusing to reach a door I couldn't go through for a second day, I hacked and tromped and twisted and pushed through the heat of the day and thick brush and jagged branches. When all of a sudden, in the middle of my best Indiana Jones imitation, the thought occurred to me—there are snakes in these hills—big ones, bad ones, poisonous ones, deadly ones! And I hate snakes (thanks, Dad for bequeathing me your worst nightmare)! I had just been reading a local guide book the night before, and looking at pictures of snake after snake, all the while taking in the grisly details of their venomous bites. And to top it off, snakes weren't the only inhabitants of these hills that could hasten my early death!

So here I am, a man on a desperate mission to reach the inspiration point of my dreams, and I am momentarily cemented in my tracks recognizing that if I were to succumb to a venomous snake bite, I could easily die here in these mountains without a soul knowing where I was. I suppose the only consolation I would have was that I died beneath my "rock of ages"!

As it turns out, it was *déjà vu* all over again! No matter how hard I tried, no matter which angle of the path I followed, no matter how many branches I grabbed onto, no matter how I stretched my legs from one stone to another—there simply was

"Sometimes You Get To The Door, But You Can't Go Through"

no reaching this magnificent promontory point. As I retreated from my defeat, all I could do was gaze up from below and behold this wonder in my imagination (and in a pencil drawing I created in my journal—which still holds a few dried tear-stains on its pages).

Sometimes you get to the door, but you can't go through.

In my mediation, I returned to that Children's Bible image of Moses and found my way to **Deuteronomy 32: 48-50.52**. Here is Moses, perched just beyond the Promised Land of his dreams, of his efforts, of his sorrow, of his prophetic acts…and he cannot enter in. All he is permitted to do is admire it, weep over it, from afar. The only taste of its milk and honey for Moses would be whatever he was able to conjure in his imagination and in the leader's heart that God had been fashioning in him since the day of burning bush encounter with *I Am* in the desert. Even for Moses, the greatest prophet of the Hebrew Testament, the father of freedom, and the only person to see God face-to-face…even for him, he now came face-to-face with one of the most challenging life lessons of all: ***Sometimes you get to the door, but you can't go through!***

I think about all the doorways whose thresholds we have stood before, and how many we have never entered, despite our best efforts and perhaps all the prayers offered on our behalf that we might indeed arrive and go through.

Nearly 16 years ago, I left Chicago and my ministry at Saint Xavier University, a ministry that I greatly loved and where I felt completely charged with a mission. But the invitation came from my religious community to *set forth* for Orlando, Florida and the pastorate of an urban, inner city parish. Now pastoring a parish, in truth doing parish work of *any kind*, had never been part of my vision for life. In fact, I avoided it like a bad rash! But here was the chance to soak up sunshine and ocean waters in Florida, and the geography was just too hard to resist.

As I prepared to depart campus ministry, teaching religion, and working in residence life, a number of things began to happen—things that my partner in campus ministry, my dear departed friend Joan Birkmann and I had worked to achieve for all of our seven years together there were finally coming to fruition! The college was in the midst of a national effort on the part of the U.S. Catholic bishops, in response to a Vatican initiative for Catholic higher education, to recapture a visible commitment to "Catholic identity". The time was ripe for a re-investment in campus ministry and the religion department. And now the fact of the matter was neither Joan nor I would taste the fruits of our hopes, dreams and efforts (Joan was also leaving the campus that same summer to move to New Orleans and get married). As we prepared to depart our beloved Chicago and Saint Xavier, Joan and I were submerged in this powerful life lesson: **Sometimes you get to the door, but you can't go through.**

This is but one instance of many where this life lesson has reared its head; and I am sure you can name your own. Sometimes this lesson sounds like:

"I've done everything I can…but the situation isn't changing!"

"We came all this way…and now it's over…and that's supposed to be it?"

"All my hard work…and for what?"

"By the way, thanks for all your help…but I wish you'd mind your own business!"

"After everything I've done for her…and this is this is the 'thanks' I get!"

"Sometimes You Get To The Door, But You Can't Go Through"

And it is precisely here that the Gospel challenge emerges. Fr. Thomas Ryan, C.S.P., in his book *Four Steps to Spiritual Freedom (Paulist Press, 2003)* speaks about the clarion call of Jesus to **relinquish the fruits**. In other words, we are challenged by the Gospel to let go of results, while at the same time, according to Ryan, giving our best to every undertaking without insisting that the results (going through the doorway) work out the way I want or demand, or even without insisting that the effort be pleasant, or fulfilling or "complete." He contrasts this *relinquishing the fruits* with our usual choice to **renounce the fruits**! When we get to the door and cannot go through, we often find ourselves saying things like:

"Who cares that it didn't work out; I wasn't really trying that hard."
"Why am I always the one who gets rejected?"
"Go ahead; let it happen the way you want…I hope it all falls apart!"

In my disappointment that the flowers were about to bloom at Saint Xavier in ways I had only dreamt of (along with the things I mentioned earlier, I was also desperately being asked to stay on the religion faculty; my colleagues were desperately trying to find a way for me to be hired as a full-time faculty member rather than as an adjunct—something I had desired for years!), I could have easily resorted to the "well, I hope it all falls apart after we leave! That'll teach them what they lost!" But in that moment, I was somehow able to *relinquish the fruits* rather than *renounce* them, and to recognize that **sometimes you get to the door, but you can't go through.**

What I believe to be true, but still struggle to practice in daily life, is that God is always working, always moving in life-giving ways…leading us to many thresholds. We are a pilgrim people, a people on a continuous journey, and we are invited to trust that God is indeed active in *both* our entrances and our leavings. And these places of our letting go, these doorways of which we are merely allowed to toe their thresholds, can be as much a blessing and as grace-filled as any of our efforts to go through the other side. The ultimate Gospel challenge, of course, is to lay hold of this truth even when we don't see it, know it for sure, desire it completely, experience it, or doubt it greatly. In the words of Thomas Ryan, **God is always ripening!**

There will always be tent rocks in the distance, inspiration ledges we cannot scale, people who don't respond to our love and affection, sicknesses that won't be healed, scars that never fade, and dreams only tasted in our imaginations. For the truth is: **Sometimes you get to the door, but you can't go through.**

Life Lesson:

"If You Want To Make A Change, You May Need To Tell A Different Story"

"If You Want To Make A Change, You May Need To Tell A Different Story"

I have met people in my life upon whom I have conferred the label "storytellers." In some of those cases, that's a compliment; in others, it's not!

I knew a young college student by the name of "Carlo" who in my mind, at the tender age of 21, was already a consummate storyteller—of the non-complimentary brand. Carlo spent late nights weaving his path through the floors of the residence hall, working his way into any room with an open door (which normally included my apartment, since the door was almost always ajar), and plying his spectacular accounts of various events, many of which had to do with his own stellar accomplishments. Most people simply ignored Carlo; but there were those who became so irritated with his exaggerated storytelling, that they told him to bug off! Personally, I liked Carlo, and although I decided early on that 98% of what he waxed on about was over-the-top, mostly made up, and with little basis in reality, I found him energetic and entertaining, and all together quite harmless.

Sometimes the designation "storyteller" means that a person knows how to stretch the truth. They are usually given to large, expansive, and often quite engaging tales about their own

"If You Want To Make A Change, You May Need To Tell A Different Story"

or others' exploits, but something in the way they lay out their stories tips us off that they are spinning fiction with a "capital F"!

Then there are those other mesmerizing storytellers who mix wonderful cocktails of fact and fiction, and as we drink in their potent elixirs, we know ourselves to be experiencing great truths about life. Unlike most peoples' reactions to Carlo, we do more than tolerate their presence among us—we relish their presence and their stories. Somehow, true storytellers open windows for our souls, so that the Spirit of God can float in an out, enlightening us and empowering us for life!

For most ancient cultures, including those laying claim to the Judeo-Christian story, a thriving oral tradition is what kept their people alive and secure in the deep memory of values and beliefs. And this is certainly true of the Native American Pueblo Indian cultures.

Surveying the pottery, jewelry, bead work, carving, weaving and sand paintings lining the blankets of the Native peoples who inhabit "El Portal," or the "front porch" of the Palace of the Governors, I spied some of the most whimsical caricatures crafted in clay and paint I had ever seen in my numerous art travels. The Palace of the Governors is the oldest continuously-occupied public building in the United States, dating all the way back to 1610. The daily market established under its plaza-facing façade serves to protect, preserve and promote authentic traditional Southwest Native American arts and crafts.

The fascinating figurines are known as Pueblo "Storytellers," a fairly recent creation in the history of Native American artistry. The first sculpture is attributed to Helen Cordero in 1964. Helen, a resident of the Cochiti Pueblo, which sits along the banks of the Rio Grande River between Santa Fe and Albuquerque, crafted her storyteller to represent her grandfather, a masterful tribal storyteller, who preserved the values and moorings of his Native culture through his gift for engaging tales of life in the pueblo.

Storyteller dolls or figurines can be male or female, and some are even populated by clowns or animals. Sometimes the storytelling elder is holding something important to the pueblo—pottery, rugs, or drums. Strikingly, storyteller dolls from the Jemez, New Mexico Pueblo are frequently holding watermelons!

And always, the central figure, the "storyteller" is surrounded by "story-listeners"—all who have their mouths gaping open! Forming almost perfect circles, their mouths are what immediately drew my attention. With the male or female storyteller firmly planted in the middle of the sculpture, the listeners, normally children, are sitting, or more accurately *hanging from* the body of their teacher! As we say, the listeners are *hanging on every word*!

I believe we are never too old for stories, as the following illustration demonstrates. As I tooled around the corner of the long hallway, with lots of people scurrying about and the level of noise reaching a fever pitch, the distinct sounds of someone reading a story pierced the clatter and pulled me in. I stood at the doorway to the room and was immediately touched by the expressive voice and face of the storyteller. Apparently, the listeners, for the most part, were equally mesmerized and responded, each in their own limited ways, when asked a question about what they had just heard. "Does anyone here know what a 'daisy' is? Can anybody remember picking flowers in a garden? Is it hard to get dirt out from under your fingernails?"

Not knowing the title of the book being read aloud, but making a quick judgment from the questions being posed, I assumed it was a child's tale about gardening, or perhaps some metaphor

"If You Want To Make A Change, You May Need To Tell A Different Story"

for "growing up."

The storyteller sat in the middle of the crowd, with book opened and propped to her side, as she made sure to show the extravagant pictures that some marvelous illustrator had created for the text.

As is always the case when it comes to storytelling, not all the listeners were able to follow along or respond to the storyteller—some were drifting away in their own worlds, with their own stories being played out; some were more concerned about the streamers hanging from the ceiling or the location of their chairs. But for the most part, many mouths were opened in broad smiles, and there were twinkling eyes scattered throughout the room.

A beautiful sight and sound indeed…but it did not take place where you may be imagining this happened. I wasn't careening through the hallways of a neighborhood daycare or elementary school. No, I was on my way after visiting and anointing a dying patient at a local nursing home.

You see no matter our age or condition, we are never too old for stories!

Ah yes, the power of stories and storytellers—they can help us breathe in new worlds of vision, or strangle us by wrapping us in only one world of vision. They can reveal hidden secrets that people work hard to keep out of sight, or they can throw up barriers that prevent us from seeing and knowing the truth. Stories and storytellers have the power to expand our minds and hearts, or they can spin tales that only seek to constrict our minds and hearts.

But the art of storytelling is not limited to characters like Carlo, or to great poets and writers, or even to the elders in every culture. *Storytelling* is so fundamental to the human experience that John and Mary Harrell in *To Tell of Gideon* assert that "storytelling is so natural to human beings it suggests a definition [of what it means to be "human"]: **we are the creatures who think in stories.**" By our very nature, we are all storytellers—and we can exercise the art of our "storytelling" as compliment or condemnation.

John Shea, a masterful storyteller himself, tells us:

> *Humankind is addicted to stories. No matter our mood, in reverie or expectation, panic or peace, we can be found stringing together incidents and unfolding episodes. We tell our stories to live* (Stories of God, 7-8).

Perhaps we don't often think about it this way, but we are surrounded every day by "stories"—they are being told by co-workers, spouses, children, friends, teachers, television programs and advertisements, radio gab-shows, media entertainment that parades around as "news," magazines, and Internet "bloggers," just to name a few.

And no less a potent source of storytelling is our Christian faith tradition. Not simply the parables of Jesus or the tales of God's activities in both testaments of sacred Scripture count as stories of faith, but our music, art, worship, creeds, rituals, practices of piety, indeed the very stories that are "told" by the choices and decisions we make in living the Gospel of Jesus Christ each day—also make each of us storytellers of God in Christ, with the Holy Spirit as the muse who inspires and infuses our storytelling.

We come by our storytelling as Christians quite naturally, as God seems to be always dishing some story for us to consume!

"If You Want To Make A Change, You May Need To Tell A Different Story"

In Psalm 81:10, we read: *Open your mouth wide and I will fill it (NRSV)*.

Human beings are not the only ones who love to fashion our lives through stories—so does our Creator God! Again, John Shea points out:

> *God not only loves to hear our stories, he loves to tell his own. And, quite simply, we are the story God tells. Our very lives are the words that come from his mouth (Stories of God, 8).*

The prophet Ezekiel speaks of being on the receiving end of the Word of God in the most literal of fashions:

So I opened my mouth, and he gave me the scroll to eat. He said to me, Mortal, eat this scroll that I give you and fill your stomach with it. Then I ate it; and in my mouth it was as sweet as honey (3:2-3 NRSV). Or better yet, in the more colorful translation of Eugene Peterson, God tells the prophet to *make a meal out of it (The Message)*!

But here's the problem, the challenge—in most cases, the stories of God in Christ are regularly muscled out by the often louder and more annoying storytellers who surround us. Indeed, the story of the Gospel way of life of Jesus Christ is increasingly an ALTERNATIVE story to the ones that fill every crack of our lives.

One Sunday, the deacon preaching at my parish called attention to "stories"—the first, an elaborate Sunday spread in the *Orlando Sentinel* about a mega-mansion of 90,000 (!) square feet being constructed in Orange County and the story of the *doyen* of that palatial dwelling—which he then juxtaposed with a second story published the next day in the *Sentinel* about the "changing faces of the homeless" and the *Orlando Rescue Mission's* efforts to keep pace (which they cannot, turning away 30-40 families, mostly women and children, each day). Now, which of the "stories" is the one the people of God might be called to pay attention to in light of the Gospel of Christ? Which story really deserves more "press" when viewed from the perspective of God and God's desires for people?

Here's the question: how bold, courageous, committed is our telling of the *alternative* stories of Jesus Christ, the ones which go against the grain of the rest of the world's storytellers? Are the "Carlos" of the world drowning out the alternative ways of seeing and being in the world which God intends for creation, drowning out the stories of Jesus Christ that literally turn the world upside down when they are proclaimed?

Many years ago, a rather famous commentator on culture, Ivan Illich, an Austrian priest and philosopher, was asked, what is the most revolutionary way to change society? His answer was both thoughtful and thought provoking: "If you want to change society, **then you must tell an alternative story**."

As the ancient ones knew so well, and have now bequeathed this life lesson to us: ***If you want to make a change, you may need to tell a different story!***

And perhaps this is why so little in our world seems to change, whether on the local, national, or international stages—or on the stages where you and I act out our daily decisions!

There are great risks to those who tell stories that are contrary to the expectations that others want us to meet—we have no further than the prophets and the Lord Jesus himself to see the usual fate that awaits people who dare spin stories that ask people

"If You Want To Make A Change, You May Need To Tell A Different Story"

to see behind the curtains, to imagine new responses to age old questions, to propose alternative actions to the dominating ones currently in use.

But this is the legacy of storytelling that Jesus Christ leaves his followers, his disciples. While we may bind up the stories of the Bible into "Children's" editions, there is hardly anything "childish" about the power and consequences of the stories of God's working in and working on God's creation!

As Christians, we are wrapped up in the eternal drama of our Storytelling God, who most beautifully brought God's story to life in the person of Jesus the Christ. As followers of this Jesus, his story becomes our story—we try to locate ourselves in the twists and turns of his life, death and resurrection. This is what the Easter mysteries are all about.

It is not by accident or coincidence that on the road to Emmaus, as the disheartened disciples tell their story of tragedy and defeat to the unknown stranger who draws near to accompany them, the stranger first opens the Scriptures, the stories of God, before revealing his true identity. Jesus takes their lonely and disconnected tale and joins it with his story and the great story of God's desires for creation. Jesus gives flesh to something Isaak Dinesen once remarked: *Any sorrow can be borne if a story can be told about it.*

The Emmaus disciples are no longer alone in their misery and grief, but are now gathered into the heart of God. After nourished by Jesus in word and table, they now have the strength to go on and to create more stories with their lives through what they have witnessed. And this is exactly what they do. Not content with merely hearing a great story, they break out from Emmaus and return to the city to proclaim good news—to reopen the story they thought had come to an end.

Long ago, a prophet named Jeremiah, who clearly was anything but enamored of his call to tell alternative stories to those who would rather hear the distorted ones of power, eventually came to declare: *Your words were found, and I ate them, and your words became to me a joy and the delight of my heart (15:16 NRSV).*

What kinds of stories are you listening to these days? What kinds of stories are you telling? Do they sound like all the rest? Or are your stories ones that will turn the world upside down as God intends?

If you find yourself stuck, unable to see new alternatives, take new initiatives, cope with a nagging problem, or breathe some fresh air, perhaps you can return to the narrative you've been telling, the story you've been relating to describe your situation, relationship, or experience. Perhaps it's time to seek the wisdom of the *Great Storyteller*, whose words always provide a feast! Sometimes it's simply a matter of living into this powerful life lesson: ***If you want to make a change, you may need to tell a different story!***

Life Lesson:

"WHEN EVERYONE IS LOOKING FOR YOU, SOMETIMES IT'S BEST TO RUN THE OTHER WAY!"

"When Everyone Is Looking For You, Sometimes It's Best To Run The Other Way!"

My musical tastes have been known to vary quite dramatically in the course of my life, or for that matter, in the course of any singular trip in the car! I enjoy a wide range of musical genres, and now with the luxury of Sirius-XM satellite radio—it's all there for the taking. The appeal of any particular type of musical genre on any given day or at any given moment has more to do with my mood or feelings than with the style or quality of the artist(s) performing the selections. There are some exceptions, though; I am *never* in the mood for acid rock, hard-core rap, operatic arias, or soft-core country and western. I mention my musical preferences because I am almost embarrassed to admit that at one time, I actually listened to and enjoyed John Denver's music! (The only thing more embarrassing I can think of would be to admit that I listened to and enjoyed Barry Manilow's music—which I did not!)

I was reminded of this strange persuasion while preparing for a piece I was set to do for an eighth grade retreat. Each year that I served as pastor of St. Andrew Church in Orlando, I shared a meditation with the soon-to-be-graduating eighth graders using an image drawn from the prophet Ezekiel, whereby God promises

"When Everyone Is Looking For You, Sometimes It's Best To Run The Other Way!"

to replace our "hearts of stone with hearts of flesh" (Ezekiel 36). During the meditation, each participant holds a stone in the palm of his or her hand while I reflect upon the ways in which we live our lives more like stones than human beings; the meditation ultimately leads to an invitation to turn over our hearts of stone and to embrace the renewed hearts that God offers to those who seek forgiveness and reconciliation. As an introduction to this meditation, while the young people are selecting their "pet rocks," the old Simon and Garfunkel tune, *I Am a Rock* plays in the background.

Lest you think I've lost track of my thoughts: okay, so what about John Denver? How do we get from Simon and Garfunkel to the "Good 'Ole Country Boy"? Simple…the aging home-made CD upon which I have recorded the S & G tune also contains a John Denver piece: *Looking for Space*.

So, I accidently bumped into John Denver while trying to locate the tune I needed for the retreat. As I listened to the opening words of *Looking for Space*, I began to reminisce about why I still had the recording. It was a favorite of mine many years beforehand when I had somewhat of a famous reputation for putting together what were then the "high-tech" presentations of their day—slide shows! This John Denver song was a staple, and a great one at that, for setting the tone for the beginning of a retreat. After all, isn't the opportunity of going on retreat nothing short of a specific way of *looking for space*, looking for desperately needed space in the midst of our otherwise hectic and confusing lives?

Allow me to share the refrain from Denver's *Looking for Space:*

*And I'm looking for space,
and to find out who I am.
And I'm looking to know and understand.
It's a sweet, sweet dream…
Sometimes I'm almost there.
Sometimes I fly like an eagle,
And sometimes I'm deep in despair.*

There is a profound life lesson here: **When everyone is looking for you, sometimes it's best to run the other way!**

As I have come to embrace the *Land of Enchantment* as my own place for retreat, both spiritual and recreational, it is clear that precisely the *space* of its landscape is central to its allure. When everyone is looking for me, or for that matter when anyone is looking for me, I too have needed to run the other way—and often that run takes me to New Mexico.

The very words "New Mexico landscape," even for those who have never had the privilege and emotional experience of setting foot on the land, immediately conjures up a mental image of other-worldly, dramatic, and eerie beauty. Desert canyons, plateaus, mountains, plains, river beds, arroyos, deciduous forests, mesas— the landscape literally *talks back to me*, and not to be the boorish guest, I respond! For the last 120 miles of flight before dropping over the mountains to land at the Albuquerque Sunport, there is nothing but sweeping, dramatic space and austere beauty. As the plane descends from the heavens, I have often felt that I melt into the vastness of the landscape and its scenic treasures.

The artist Ernest Blumenschien, himself mesmerized by the palette that awaited his artistry in New Mexico and one of the pioneer artists of the Taos movement, once wrote this description:

"When Everyone Is Looking For You, Sometimes It's Best To Run The Other Way!"

The beautiful Sangre de Cristo...stretching away from the foot of the range was a vast plateau cut by the Rio Grande and by lesser gorges in which were located small villages of flat-roofed adobe houses built around a church and plaza, all fitting into the color scheme of the tawny surroundings. The sky was clear, clean blue with sharp moving clouds. The color, the effective character of the landscape, the drama of the vast spaces, the superb beauty and serenity of the hills, stirred me deeply (Bickerstaff, Pioneer Artists of Taos, 1955, 30-31).

If we're honest, all of us spend a good bit of our time *looking for space*, but rarely finding it. Too often we believe that when people are looking for us, we need to respond to them as quickly and completely as possible. Our world is crowded. While we may not suffer under the population crunch of China, or find ourselves crammed into oppressively constricted living spaces in shanty towns, as much of our world is, we are crowded by obligations, commitments, too few hours and enormous expectations—both for ourselves and others. We find ourselves crowded by heartaches and disappointments, financial pressures and medical bills, material belongings and desires. Through it all, we keep looking for space; we keep attempting to carve our niches where we won't be bothered, where others will be safely and securely far enough away from us that we can breathe freely. Unfortunately, once we seem to find a space, it doesn't take long before someone or something else discovers this same niche and brings the crowd along! Our spaces don't remain sacred for long. So we start up again, looking for that elusive *space*, which, in John Denver's words, may only be a "sweet, sweet, dream." Although elusive, *sacred space* **must** be found for our emotional, physical, intellectual, and certainly our spiritual health, which is simply the other three combined and placed in relationship with God.

Truth is…***when everyone is looking for you, sometimes it's best to run the other way!***

Jesus was no stranger to the quest for *looking for space*. Throughout the Gospel accounts, we see Jesus stealing away, either alone or in the company of his closest, most intimate companions. In Mark's account, the opening chapter provides us with a whirlwind of activity as Jesus enters into his public ministry. In the space of 34 lines, Jesus proclaims the Gospel of repentance, calls his first disciples, cures a demoniac and Simon's mother-in-law, as well as engages in numerous other healings. It's no wonder that we learn in verse 35, *rising early before dawn, he left and went off to a deserted place, where he prayed.* However, within a short while, it is Simon, always the impetuous one, who tracks down Jesus and announces that *everyone is looking for you!* Simon, as well as the rest of Jesus' apostles, would learn over and over again, that "retreat" is an essential dimension of their relationship with God and the work in which Jesus is inviting them to share. The classic prescription for sacred space, reminiscent of the doctor's orders to "take two of these and call me in the morning," comes by way of invitation from Jesus: **Come by yourselves to a deserted place and rest a while (Mark 6:31a).** Translation: **When everyone is looking for you, sometimes it's best to run the other way!**

Borrowing language common to Eastern and even Native American spiritualities, we often lose our *center* as we spin our way through life. Very often, the centrifugal force of our life encounters launches us away from our center and out to the edges,

"When Everyone Is Looking For You, Sometimes It's Best To Run The Other Way!"

where we find ourselves desperately clinging with white-knuckled intensity. We are challenged to find that sacred space which allows us a return to our center, to that place where we can gain some clarity away from the *sadness and the screams*. John Denver melodically describes it this way:

> *All alone in the universe,*
> *sometimes that's how it seems.*
> *I get lost in the sadness and the screams.*
> *Then I look in the center;*
> *suddenly everything's clear.*
> *I find myself in the sunshine and my dreams.*

The quest for sacred space, for that secure environment where we can afford ourselves the *luxury* of reflection, doesn't always need to lead us far from home—or all the way to New Mexico! Often, it may be within the confines of our own regular space that we carve out a sacred niche. It's not uncommon to hear a parent speak of "quality" space as close as (yet most times as difficult to commandeer as) one's unoccupied bathroom!

I can recall an occasion when I had the opportunity to take some desperately needed time away, and I found refuge from my parish ministry in downtown Winter Park! Although only a mere 10 miles away from home, I may as well have been 210 miles away—the results would have been the same, I believe. The ability to get away from my normal surroundings and demands did wonders in refreshing my spirit. I know that not only my own self, but every person I come in contact with is far better served with a "renewed" me than with a tired, cranky and dejected me. Physical space is intimately connected with emotional, intellectual, and spiritual space. Creating physical space between us and the demands and responsibilities of our lives is crucial if we are to be re-charged emotionally, intellectually and spiritually.

Unfortunately, we continue to speak about the *necessity* of this space as *luxury*. Given this attitude, we only underline the fact that our priorities are out of whack, and that we are continuing to damage our health. The reasons for this way of thinking differ slightly between individuals. I personally know these "reasons" well, for at one time or another, they have served me with all their might.

Some of us just "need to be needed"; we gain our sense of self-worth through constant performance. Some of us feel "guilty" when we are "wasting time on ourselves"; we mistake aloneness with loneliness, and we quickly set out to fill up our environment with something or someone. Some of us are afraid we'll "miss something"; we seemingly make an imaginary return to the days of our early teens when we couldn't stand the thought, let alone the reality of being away from our friends for fear that something important would happen in our absence.

Some of us have not nurtured the skills necessary to "reflect" upon our lives; we secretly hold that "too much thinking" is dangerous and just confuses us. It's another version of that ill-fated syndrome: "what-you-don't-know-can't-hurt-you" (but oh my, YES it can!). Some of us are afraid of what we might discover about ourselves, God or others if we take the time to scratch below the surface living we're usually engaged in. We fear there is some "monster" hiding just beyond our view, so we make sure our "view" goes no further than the tip of our nose.

Some of us have gotten so accustomed to caring for others' needs before our own, and these "others" have a significant

"When Everyone Is Looking For You, Sometimes It's Best To Run The Other Way!"

investment in us thinking this way since *they* stand to lose if we step back for a breather (whether we're speaking of our boss, our children, our spouse, our aging parents, our fellow committee members); we're simply out of practice or out of touch with even naming our own needs, so much so that we hesitate even speaking them outside the secret musings of our own hearts, let alone actually setting out to respond to them.

Yes, our "reasons" for avoiding or side-stepping our need for sacred space, for running in the other direction, may vary, but the *necessity* that we look and find such sacred space is common to us all.

It seems that in the course of our praxis for striving to be people of faith in Jesus Christ, we quickly focus upon certain commandments of the Lord—especially those dealing with "shall nots." Perhaps we would better serve the Lord, and in return the wonderful creatures God has made of each of us, if we were to focus on the "thou shalts," particularly Jesus' admonition to *come to an out of the way place*. What would happen in the days and weeks ahead if we made this invitation the focus of our attention? What would happen if we occupied our thinking and our anxiety about being faithful to the Lord with an "examination of conscience" concerning the ways in which have *not* searched for sacred space, for the ways we have *not* taken a path toward space that allows us to be rejuvenated in spirit and flesh? What would happen if we "feared" Jesus' judgment upon us if it were based upon the quality of time spent luxuriating with the Lord in holy space that is unoccupied with all the trappings of our lives and work, but rather is filled with nothing and no one but our deepest selves and God?

What kind of *space* are you currently looking for, or would you allow yourself to look for if you were to be so kind to yourself?

What would it take to make a regular habit of securing sacred space for resting? Who might need to help you? What might you need to ask someone else (recognizing that people do not seem to hesitate to *ask you* for what *they* need) to secure the sacred space that's crucial to your own health? With what must you wrestle in order to gain a better perspective on your own need for holy space?

Jesus knew the importance and necessity of returning to the center, even as the crowds and his apostles chased him from one corner of Galilee to the other. I contend that Jesus may be the author of this life lesson under consideration. Not unlike you and me, Jesus seemingly had to "steal" these moments amidst the onrush of extremely pressing needs, yet he made it a priority to visit sacred space. He knew that without those visits, he would shrivel and dry up. All too familiar with the prophet Ezekiel's vision of the *dry bones*, I am certain that Jesus knew that without periodic retreats to his space of rejuvenation and restoration, he would end up becoming one more dry bone of spent good intentions and incredibly compassionate care strewn upon the landscape of human affairs.

Jesus is calling each of us by name…only this time, he's not asking us to *do* another task for him; rather he's asking us to do something *for ourselves. Come by yourself to a deserted place and rest a while.* In other words: **When everyone is looking for you, sometimes it's best to run the other way!**

Life Lesson:

"IN THE MENAGERIE OF LIFE, GOD IS NO KITTEN"

"In The Menagerie Of Life, God Is No Kitten"

The fact that I am even proposing this particular life lesson stands as testimony to the power of good writing over my own personal distastes! Anyone who knows me knows that "in the menagerie of life," my attraction to animals is extremely limited…and the greatest of those limitations relates to *cats*! I was the one, back in the late 1980s, who received as a birthday gift from some pesky, but insightful teenager, the bottom half of a stuffed "Garfield"-looking animal that was meant to be hung, upside down, from beneath my front car bumper! I did, in fact, proudly attach and display it in order to give absolute testimony that cats sat atop *the* golden throne within the pantheon of my personal dislikes. So with a big gulp (and the honesty that tells you I haven't changed my mind about felines), let me set forth this life lesson!

Every once in awhile, I come across in my reading a phrase that ignites a powerful image, which causes me to look a little more deeply at myself and the things in my world. In a world that is filled with words, multiplying nearly at the speed of sound, it seems to take a lot more than it used to in order to make me sit up and take notice of someone's writing, to be truly moved by their words. I often think the same thing about my own writing! The curse of every writer, the burden that we all bear, is that we

"In The Menagerie Of Life, God Is No Kitten"

recognize all too readily that the words we put to print are just so many more jottings in an already overwhelming pile of verbiage. So frequently, my thinking is—why write? Lord knows there's enough of it out there already. In all honesty, someone has probably already said what I'm about to say (and probably has said it much better!), so why should I bother? Why should I think that anyone wants to read what I have to say?

And, as every writer knows, the answer to this last question isn't very comforting nor satisfying, but it's the only one that keeps echoing in our souls—we write because we have to—it's etched in the depths of our spirits!

While on retreat in New Mexico one summer, I read a wonderful little spiritual "diary" by Nancy Malone called *Walking the Literary Labyrinth*. In her thin-paged, but deeply touching tome, she recounts significant events in her life and how certain passages of books or poems she was reading at the time guided her through these events. The subtitle of her book is *A Spirituality of Reading*. While making my way through her reflections—out jumped a powerful image that has been rolling around in my head and heart since that hot, desert afternoon when I first encountered it. It was to become the source of this life lesson: **In the menagerie of life, God is no kitten!**

Malone quotes a revered writer on prayer, Orthodox Archbishop Anthony Bloom, who delivers an intriguing and unsettling image of God in his book *Beginning to Pray*:

> *To meet God means to enter the* **cage of a tiger**—*it is not a pussycat that you meet—it's a tiger. The realm of God is dangerous. You must enter it and not just seek information about it (102).*

What a compelling image that makes me rethink my oftentimes lackadaisical approach to speaking with and relating to God! What seems to happen in the course of our prayer life is that we get stuck with particular images and experiences of God which, while they may make us all warm and fuzzy inside, place incredible limitations on God and our experience of God. We begin to think and believe that God can actually *be limited* to the specific ways in which I think about God or experience God. As an insightful author once penned, our God becomes "too small" *(Your God Is Too Small, J. B. Phillip)*! We tend to run away from or dismiss those unsettling images of God, which force us to push out our boundaries about who God is and how God relates to us and to our world.

Bloom's image allows God to come alive in my spirit as more than a pacifier of my dis-ease, or a warm blanket to wrap around my despair. Rather God becomes someone with whom I tangle, with whom I wrestle (much the same as did Jacob when he "wrestled with the angel"), and someone who is to be taken seriously!

Nancy Malone, in her reflecting upon the words of Anthony Bloom, takes the image one step further, as she relates the difficulties through which she was passing at a particular stage of her life. In wrestling with God during a struggle with alcohol and medications for depression, Malone says that she indeed "entered the cage of the tiger" and felt ***flayed*** by it! Another amazing, insightful use of words and imagery!

To be *flayed* literally means to "strip off the skin or the surface of something, to strip of possession." To encounter God in prayer is not always about comfort and consolation, about the mending of our wounds. At times, an encounter with God is meant to strip away all of our surface and superficial living, and expose the core of who we are and where our choices and decisions are taking us. Encountering our "tiger-God" in prayer is about deeper, clearer *revelation*, and not simply covering up what we do not want to see, to admit to, or believe about others or ourselves. Entering "the cage" is dangerous—but the kind of danger that pushes us to an edge, where we can be invited to see and encounter a deeper, richer, more vibrant God than the one we have been neatly packaging for our own purposes.

Anthony Bloom's dynamic image/experience of God, and Nancy Malone's reflection upon encountering the "tiger-God" in her own spiritual journey helps me to see, once again, that I am not the one intended to be "in control" of God, but that God is the one who calls the shots—and placing myself in a vulnerable, dangerous, unsettling position before God can be the beginning of a more fervent love of God.

In this sense for me, the words of Bloom and Malone are truly prophetic. They have done what poet Gerard Manley Hopkins called for in his own intriguing way:

> *Let me now*
> *Jolt*
> *Shake and unset your mortised metaphors.*

I am thankful, today, for writers like Bloom and Malone who risk speaking to me and others an uncomfortable word and image, so that we might move a bit off our center and take a fresh look at God and our relationship with God. I am thankful for the life lessons that spring from the power of the written word. I am thankful for this life lesson: **In the menagerie of life, God is no kitten!**

Poetic Interlude

"THE ADOBE DESERT CHAPEL"
THE CHAPEL OF THE
BAPTIST IN THE DESERT
Prémontré 1120/Santa Maria de la Vid 2000

(An adaptation from a poem by Edwina Gateley entitled "The Hermitage" in Psalms of a Laywoman)

It is welcomingly dark in this adobe brick sanctuary.
The high desert night is silent and utterly still,
save the distant hum of passing cars on the road below.
There is only a slight flicker from the red sanctuary lamp
casting warmth across the body and visage of San Damiano above.
Shadows play across the viga beams—
solid and glistening with varnish.
And a night swallow swoops between the piñons
framing the corner windows beyond the nicho.
Too warm yet to ignite the kiva fireplace—
but it stands ready.
Logs piled from a leftover season, looking for that first gust of winter
    chill so to be called to duty.
Aspens and cottonwoods crackle in the distance, instead of flaming
    logs—
which is enough for this time and place.
Icons with their gold leaf are illuminated too—
hung upon the adobe walls, surrounding me actually—

Mary
the Baptist
Norbert too.
The ample Jemez pottery pregnant—
holding within it—
the Light that visits this darkness.

It is beautiful and lovely here,
nakedly simple, overwhelming security,
with rustic necessities, so as not to complicate
Encounter.

There is a kinship between my soul
and these dry, earthy, protective stones
that make this wayside shelter—
this refuge—
comforting and safe.
I share a peace and integrity
with the lamp, the icons, the swallow, the night—
and the bits and pieces of desert sand and stones
dragged from the winding path leading here—
insistent symbols, each and all of
Incarnation.

I've come apart—to be a part—
from the everyday action and interplay
of life.
I've come apart,
but remain a part,
for there is no escaping

Incarnation
No matter how much I desire it or try it.
My work, my ministry, my incessant commitments—
and all their feverish movement
exist—in this moment—as memories
and we—the lamp, the icons, the swallow, the night, and the Mystery
all the bits and pieces—
are woven here together
on this mesa—this expansive table-land—
in the vast and silent desert—where
Encounter
is most likely given birth.

Benjamin Berinti
Norbertine Retreat at Santa Maria de la Vid, Albuquerque, NM
September 21, 2011

Life Lesson:

"IN ORDER TO SEE THE STARS, YOU HAVE TO LOOK UP!"

"In Order To See The Stars, You Have To Look Up!"

How often have I wandered out on a strikingly clear night and been immediately *enchanted,* drawn to *look up at the sky* as though a giant magnetic force were locked upon the steel in my eyes, lifting my gaze upward, beyond the intricacies of my present circumstances? How often has this happened to you?

Perhaps it isn't too often, as many of us live in areas that inhibit the beauty of the night sky by the cast-off of all our electrical, artificial night light. Not that all the glitter and glow of towns and cities, which turns darkness into day, doesn't have its own attractive beauty. Just look out the window of an airliner as you float the final 10,000 feet on your nighttime arrival into the airport. But on a gorgeous star-lit night, twinkling specks pinned against the black drapery of the heavens, something within me cries out to dim the glare and to allow the celestial wonder before my eyes to work its magic in my soul.

Such was not the case as I sat on my roundhouse front porch, in the middle of the pitch black night outside Jemez Springs, New Mexico, preparing to wind down a powerful encounter with God and myself during my annual retreat.

There is something mysteriously seductive about a night sky, radiant with glittering luminaries, poking through like pinholes

"In Order To See The Stars, You Have To Look Up!"

pricked in a massive blanket of darkness. What wonders have been beheld in the face of such a heavenward gaze? What hopes and dreams have been born underneath such a splendid canopy? What promises and commitments have seeped out as such a night sky has enveloped tired and confused hearts—giving them the stamina before the unknown or inexperienced?

In 1960, the ailing and depleted great American author John Steinbeck, writing of his final voyage across the country, is struck by the power of a starlit desert:

> *All night in this waterless air [of desert] the stars come down just out of reach of your fingers. In such a place lived the hermits of the early church piercing to infinity with unlittered minds. The great concepts of oneness and of majestic order seem always to be born in the desert. The quiet counting of the stars, and observation of their movements, came first from desert places* (Travels with Charley: In Search of America, 1962).

No matter our vantage point in attempting to swallow a night sky in all its wondrous array; no matter how magnetically attractive the stars may be, there is one simple truth about the stars. No matter how powerful their allure, ***in order to see the stars, you have to look up!***

When was the last time you *looked up at the sky*? When was the last time you raised your eyes beyond the mundane and all-consuming expectations and demands of the moment, whatever those demands may look like in your life? When was the last time you looked up within a faith community and allowed God to welcome you and the community into a brighter, clearer, more splendid vision of your baptismal faith, into a renewed sense of who you are as a community of believers, into the dream that is always being rekindled by the fires of a Holy Spirit, the Spirit of God who continues to rejuvenate, transform and transfigure the world and its inhabitants?

Echoing the words of Steinbeck, small wonders and great visions have been born simply by following the directive to *look up*. Our ancestors in faith, Abram and Sarah were invited by God to cast their tired, weary, aged, and surely impaired eyes upon a magnificent desert night sky, and to begin the impossible task of numbering the stars. Tired, weary and aged though they were, they trusted in the Lord's command; they fixed their gaze upon that sky—and because they did so, the seed of a great nation was sown, a nation whose descendants we are—the holy and chosen ones of God! With one simple turn of their heads skyward, Abram and Sarah were introduced to the great dream of God, the dream of descendants, the dream of a fuller life beyond anything they had yet experienced, the dream of an abiding covenant with God.

John, James and Peter, as three of Jesus' most intimate companions, were invited not only to *look up at the sky*, but were, in the understanding of the ancients, literally invited *up into the sky* when Jesus took them to a mountaintop for prayer and the transformative experience that God bestowed upon Jesus in that moment. The three apostles, in the midst of prayer, were allowed to experience Jesus in his full glory and radiance as Son of God!

They like Abram and Sarah, *needed* this experience in order to renew their tired hearts and souls, to restore the glimmer of God's promises to their weary eyes. We are told by the evangelist Luke that, as they prayed, they *had been overcome by sleep*. But as the

"In Order To See The Stars, You Have To Look Up!"

radiance of the vision broke forth, as the sky wretched open and the voice called out from the cloud that descended upon them, they *became fully awake…they saw his glory*. Indeed, in the midst of their drowsiness and clenched eyes, a new awakening took place, a new vision was set forth, and this incredible experience upon the holy mountain fortified them and filled them with such joy that Peter exclaimed: *Master, it is good that we are here!*

I am certain, that as Abram clutched his wife Sarah as they held each other close in fear and wonder under that gorgeous night sky of God's grandeur, these same words fell from their feeble and desert-cracked lips: *Lord, it is good that we are here!*

But too often, in spite of the promises and renewed vision to be gained by *looking up*, we are bowed down, stuck with our vision barely at eye-level, and that's on the better days! We become so mired in our present circumstances that our vision becomes crippled, and we lose the muscle to raise our heads and look about us. As we make our way long the journey of our life, we lose sight of who we are, where we are going. We get stuck along the way; we too become frightened and feeble; we too turn our eyes downward, burdened under the day to day bumps and bruises that afflict all of us. We know all too well the path of which Jesus spoke to his apostles immediately *before* their mountain top experience--that suffering and death are inevitable, that disappointment and rejection are the stones that line the path to our own "Jerusalem". We don't even have to go looking for those things that will lower our gaze—surely they'll find their way to us on their own!

Like Abram and Sarah, we too experience our own "barrenness," our inability to give birth to all that God desires for us and our world; we too grow old and weary (and not just with the passage of biological years) under the stress of continuous hoping and dreaming; we too experience that the great "promise of the stars" often seems too far away, too remote to have the power to sustain us.

But God knew what Abram and Sarah needed…God knew that Jesus' apostles needed a transformation, a strength and courage to help them cling to their Master as his impending suffering and death loomed larger on the horizon. And God knows what we need, both in our personal lives and in the life of our families and faith communities.

The only risk, albeit a significant one, is to live into this life lesson: ***In order to see the stars, you have to look up!***

Life Lesson:

"In The Fabric Of Life, There Are Always Loose Threads"

"In The Fabric Of Life, There Are Always Loose Threads"

Every time I do it, I still look around to see who may be watching. And even though my mom lives over 1000 miles away, I sense her presence and her disappointed, forlorn stare. Seems that at 54 years old, I still *pick at* a loose thread on my sweaters!

Funny I'm not plagued by a recurrent dream where I'm tugging at some errant thread in a sweater when all of a sudden, not only my garment but my whole life unravels before my eyes! Mom would probably say, "Told you so, but you didn't listen (again)!"

In August 2004, while staying at the Redondo Retreat Center near Jemez Springs, New Mexico, the director of this spiritual ground-zero nestled in the mountains invited me to take a look at a couple of Navajo weavings she was helping sell for a friend. Small but elegant pieces, they were created by Maxine, at that time a woman in her fifties—alone with five children (one of her children suffered from spina bifida). She lived in Counselor, NM, eight miles off the highway, deep into the desert. She is an artisan who raises her own sheep, spins her own wool, makes her own dyes from the earthen plants that surround her home—and has no electricity or running water! It took her months to make one of the 3'x3' weavings I held in my hand.

"In The Fabric Of Life, There Are Always Loose Threads"

As Sharon spoke to me about Maxine, I found myself handling the weavings with a deeper reverence than at first, now gingerly fingering and gazing upon something truly "sacramental."

One of those weavings (I wish now I had purchased both of them) is draped over a small kiva ladder in the office of the spiritual development center where I now work, a daily reminder of Maxine, the dying art of Navajo weaving, and the power of human craftsmanship to connect us with the great Craftsman of Creation.

And I know something now I didn't know that beautiful August night in 2004—Navajos hate to complete anything! Baskets, rugs, blankets—Navajos never intend for their artifacts to be too perfect, too close-ended. Here's the dilemma reflected in the Navajo "secret"—a definitive ending cramps the spirit of the creator and saps the life from the art. Consequently, they leave gaps and imperfections. For the Navajo, completeness is tantamount to suffocation!

Looking at my own Navajo weaving, I'm now aware of the one (I think I may actually see more than one) clear imperfection woven into the pattern. It is precisely here that the weaver allows room for, makes space for, and creates a portal for the Spirit to move in and out of the weaving.

While I amazingly can keep my hands off the loose threads in my Navajo rug, I'm not so successful in life—and I'm not talking about cardigans now! Perhaps it is the Spirit passing in and out of Maxine's sacramental weaving that leads me to this life lesson: ***In the fabric of life, there are always loose threads!*** So much of life is unfinished business, even as we daily struggle to "tie up loose ends" or bring our projects and dreams and relationships to perfection.

During one particular visit to my parents' home in the mountains of Pennsylvania, I took a ride with my dad on the back end of our "quad" motorcycle along the forest roads surrounding their property. As we tooled by numerous cabins and camps, I noticed one of the residents was engaged in some major earth-moving around his rather large piece of land. My first thought, which I shared with my dad, was how much John's place was in a state of disarray—an incredible eyesore set amidst the otherwise majestic beauty of the forest. It was readily apparent to me that this man was a "starter" of projects rather than a "completer"! The otherwise beautiful landscape of the forest was torn up into several unfinished, incomplete, and I use the term loosely here, "projects". If it weren't for the cabin built on the property, any passerby would have imagined it to be a dumping ground! Holes, large tree roots, ditches, wood piles, half-planted saplings, mounds of rock and other unidentifiable debris littered the place.

My father confirmed my suspicions and evaluations that indeed the owner is known amongst the local town folk as relishing incompleteness, always beginning two additional projects for every one that is not yet finished.

The scene sent shivers down my spine—the kind I usually get when I witness someone cutting their spaghetti into tiny little pieces! Too many loose ends drive me crazy!

In another scenario just last weekend, while helping a friend with some decorative remodeling of a dining room, we engaged in a friendly disagreement over how much time should be spent on the project and when it would all be completed. In the face of my battle against incompleteness and the direct protestations of my friend, I insisted upon finishing what we had begun in the course of the weekend—no matter how much time it took! There

"In The Fabric Of Life, There Are Always Loose Threads"

was to be no dragging this project out over the days or weeks ahead. Once I begin a task, I always seem to push myself to its completion (or at least attempt to), having a difficult time dealing with bits and pieces that haven't yet fallen into place.

On a more serious note...when I was serving in my first pastorate, I was charged with caring for the parish grade school, amongst the many duties as pastor. I loved the school, the faculty, children and families. I recognized the school was a vibrant part of the dynamic life of our church community, while at the same time, the school was a source of constant worry—human, spiritual, and especially financial—for me and others. One of the struggles we faced over the six years of my pastorate was finding the "perfect" principal to lead the school. This life lesson was driven home day after day, despite my resistance, as we kept looking for "perfection," or some close facsimile that would give us the management and care we so desperately needed. In the six years I was pastor, we had four different principals—and I was one of them for a year! As hard as we all tried to get things to work for the good of the school and settle on a principal who could attend to our many needs, we always came up short. Many lost nights of sleep and grinding stomachs were part of the roller coaster ride we were on during those years, but the harder I (or anyone else for that matter) tried to find *the* administrator, the less successful we were. Each of the principals had their gifts and talents, and each had their critical weaknesses—but none of them were able to bring the "new spring" we so desperately desired for our parish school.

At a final point in the process, I finally recognized that "perfection" was the wrong quality to seek. While it was still important to land on an administrator who possessed many of the skills we needed in our particular environment, somehow we all had to come to the uncomfortable realization that the "perfect" principal (like the "perfect" pastor, or musician, or receptionist, or parent, or student, or fundraiser) doesn't exist. The harder we worked at seeking perfection, the more constricted, I believe, we all became in allowing room for the Spirit to truly pass through our school and parish community.

In a more mundane and less dramatic way, perhaps that's why I'm so attracted to simple household chores like vacuuming and ironing! They both involve a specific task to do, a precise method of doing those tasks, and a tremendous sense of fulfillment and *completion* when I finally get to see the perfectly starched shirt on the hanger, the nicely creased pants in the closet ready for the next occasion I put them on, or the sweeping grooves in the carpet left behind from a thorough vacuum run. There is something in me, and I suspect in many of us, that resists the Navajo sensibility that celebrates incompleteness and imperfection. I suspect I'm not alone in loving clean (literal and figurative) endings, a satisfying conclusion to every Act III, and the look of brightly wrapped, unopened packages.

Life, however, doesn't seem to work like my favorite prime-time television procedural—our school principal challenge was a far cry from an episode of *The Mentalist*; resolving the conflicting evidence in a situation at work lasts longer than the 20 minutes it takes to solve not one, but three mysteries on *CSI*. My friend Simon Baker, the Mentalist, always solves the crime, and usually with a flourish of humor and wit; the Las Vegas Crime Lab sews up every thread in those swiftly-moving stories. I'm not anywhere near as good! It's the ragged, the unfinished, and the ambiguous that seem to populate my storylines.

St. Augustine of Hippo, who himself battled with numerous

"In The Fabric Of Life, There Are Always Loose Threads"

"loose threads" in his own life journey, perhaps captured it best in his now famous words, **Our hearts are restless, O God, until they rest in thee.** We do not settle for, nor long abide with disconnected bits and pieces, loose threads. In his book *Stories of God*, author John Shea, speaking about the nature of human beings, reconfirms and elaborates on our struggle:

The fact is we can't leave anything alone. Everything we encounter is quickly and compulsively interpreted. We do not long abide experience in fragmented, chaotic form.

But isn't life a giant sweater or Navajo weaving threaded with decisions that could have been wiser, less regrettable; songs whose verses never seem to stop; faces I'll never see again; apologies or advice that comes out sideways; mathematics that doesn't add up; plans that clearly have "parts not included"; heartaches that won't fully mend; fears that still creep out from the basement closet or storage depot we've crammed them into; compassion that isn't always enough; relationships we haven't satisfied despite our best efforts and deep love for someone?

We are constantly reminded of incompleteness both within and around us, and the importance of embracing this life lesson. Around us and within our souls we see the inability of people to make life-long commitments; a disturbing lack of an abiding sense of accomplishment at work, home or school; unfulfilling personal relationships; never seeming to have the "right" skills at any given moment; constant wonderment at whether or not we have influenced another person's life in a positive way; questions of inadequacy in being a parent, spouse, or member of a church community; the ongoing battle between races and cultures; inundated with material possessions and creature-comforts, yet overcome by a gnawing sense of the need for still more; being told that what we thought was the "best" product or service is now only second rate, and that we must rush out and purchase the "new and improved" before it's too late; the unending search for "greener pastures" just beyond where we happen to be at any given moment; the constant barrage of cynicism and discontent that erupts just at the point when we think we've laid a contentious issue to rest; never being able to say "I'm sorry" enough to some people who experience hurt from us; never being able to "pay the full price" for our actions and finally being allowed to move beyond some past transgression or foolish mistake; wondering whether or not anyone will be satisfied or ready to move on after a difficult choice or decision has been made.

German theologian Karl Rahner, offering what I believe is another take on my life lesson, once wrote:

> **In the torment of the insufficiencies of everything attainable we eventually learn that here, in this life, all symphonies remain unfinished!**

This truth is in fact, in the mind of spiritual writer Ronald Rolheiser, dyed into the wool and thread of our human fabric; it's no accident. In his work *The Holy Longing: The Search for a Christian Spirituality (Doubleday, 1999)*, he writes:

> *We are forever restless, dissatisfied, frustrated, and aching…there is within us a fundamental dis-ease.… We are not easeful human beings who occasionally get restless, serene persons who once in a while are obsessed with desire. The reverse is true. We are driven persons, forever obsessed, congenitally dis-eased (3).*

"In The Fabric Of Life, There Are Always Loose Threads"

In the fabric of life, there are always loose threads.

I see a glimmer of hope, however, shining through the Evangelist John's Gospel. In Chapter 16, we find Jesus speaking with his disciples about the sending and coming of an *Advocate*. These passages are the beginning of his farewell addresses to his followers, filled with a strange combination of exhilarating anticipation and the sadness of letting go:

> *Very truly, I tell you, you will weep and mourn, but the world will rejoice; you will have pain, but your pain will turn into joy. So you have pain now; but I will see you again, and your hearts will rejoice and no one will take your joy from you.* **On that day you will not question me about anything** *(John 16: 20. 22-23a).*

My first reaction to this scripture is: Please! Let this day come soon! Let the day come when everything will fit together, all the loose threads will be gathered into one, finely woven tapestry. Let the day come when all the questions that flood our hearts and souls will be answered. Let the day come when the struggle for completion meets its end, and all things are finally threaded together in the completed garment of God's presence. Let the day come when the restlessness that inhabits at least some corner of each of our lives fades away, and we at last experience true peace and serenity—free from all distress. Let the day come when we will be so overwhelmed with sustained rather than passing joy that grief in any form will be a forgotten memory.

There is this grand, hopeful promise—but in the meantime, the fundamental questions, the unfinished business remain; what shall we do?

In the face of these loose threads, the desires and incompletion, the unfinished symphonies and recipes, do we simply bemoan the truth; retreat in despair; sink into resignation; pick away at them like someone suffering from the DTs seeing loose threads of life like crawling spiders on us? Or can we see them, as Donald McCullough so wisely revealed in his wonderful meditation *The Consolations of Imperfection: Learning to Appreciate Life's Limitations (Brazos Press, 2004)*—as *consolations,* threads of an engaging spiritual paradox?

While Jesus indeed promises a day of *no more questions*, it looks as if that day is too far away to grab hold of; yet, to the promise we still cling, for we know God and the Lord Jesus to be faithful to their promises. Until the dawn of that day, I believe I'm asked to be a little more understanding with the incompleteness of my own hopes and passions, as well as those of others; I'm invited to embrace my imperfections rather than abhor them. I'm called to know the depth of God's gifts, present within me and graciously distributed in others, which often do conspire, albeit in all too fleeting ways, to bring about moments of joy, tenderness, forgiveness, understanding, accomplishment, satisfaction and love.

I suspect I will still want nicely wrapped, easy-to-open packages (like the ones all the beautiful people on television soap operas receive at Christmas; you know, the ones where the tops just lift right off with no fuss or muss) at the end of my day—the ultimate homily every time, a fully satisfied counselee out every door, delivering the "aha" insight at the drop of a dime, a totally reconciled person exiting every sacramental confession.

Until that glorious day of *no more questions* breaks forth, I suppose I'll need to be a little less tense when driving by John's

"In The Fabric Of Life, There Are Always Loose Threads"

unfinished mountain forest lot, a little less obsessive about hanging that last strip of wallpaper in the dining room before the weekend concludes, and a whole lot more patient with the God who seeded our souls with divine restlessness.

I will still somehow keep finding my finger magnetically pulled toward every loose thread on every garment, but the life lesson I desire, the one I invite each of us to live into along with me is just this: ***In the fabric of life, there are always loose threads.***

There is real consolation, empowerment, freedom, and grace woven into this truth—as the Navajos know so well. For through the imperfections, the snags, the loose threads, and the breathing spaces, the Spirit is welcome to move in and out of our lives.

Life Lesson:

"No Matter Where You Go, Somebody's Been There Already"

"No Matter Where You Go, Somebody's Been There Already"

To say that I am thorough when packing up and getting ready to leave a hotel room is clearly an understatement. If I open some remote drawer or reach inside the closet safe once, I do it a handful of times; although most things I'm carrying could easily be replaced if I were to accidentally leave them behind (after all, once money, airline information, and wallet are secure—the rest can be dispensed with). Credit cards, although dangerous in most people's clutches, are wonderfully comforting pieces of plastic, assuring that some missing item can quickly be re-acquired (perhaps even something better than the old model) with a simple swipe of the hand.

I am determined, when checking out, not to leave as much as a trace of my presence behind. And then of course, once departed, the cleaning crew does the rest. They are charged with wiping out any vestiges of the previous guests, so that upon arrival, every newcomer has the distinct illusion that they are the first ones to ever stay in this suite. It's part of the magic of hotels. Just think about it, you can occupy the same space for a week, spread all of your life out in every nook and cranny of those pampered quarters, engage in the most personal hygienic things in the luxury bathroom, make the place feel like home—and then, in the blink of an eye (and the scrubbing bubbles of the maid), your memory is eliminated from that space, just as if you had never been there, or for that matter, ever existed! Hotel rooms, from the plushiest Ritz-Carlton grandly towering over the most magical island resort to the seediest "Hideaway Acres" wedged in between a truck stop and a worn out, beer-encrusted swill hall, are all about *passing through*—and leaving no traces behind.

One of the things I have come to love and respect about the indigenous people of North America, particularly as I have experienced the Native American pueblo cultures dotting the trail between Albuquerque and Santa Fe, New Mexico, is their profound respect for *elders*, as well as the *ancestors*. Not only does this connection appear in their ways of life, but it oozes from the land itself.

So often for people like me who visit the sacred terrain of New Mexico, one finds that the very land *speaks*. One can almost hear the ancestors, the spirits of those gone before us. Within Native American cultures, there is no sense of wiping away all traces of those who have passed this way before us, rather there is a celebration and a maintaining of those traces.

This abiding sensibility emerges as a natural consequence of the profound importance Native Americans give to *relation* as the only way of living in this world with any integrity—all epitomized in their vision of the *circle of life*. It is this sense of relation, connection, and mindfulness that inspired me to name this life lesson: **No matter where you go, somebody's been there already.**

But so often, we live and move from one space to another as though no one has ever passed this way before us. We lose our connectedness, our relationship with all that has come and gone.

In *The Sea,* a mesmerizing, lavishly penned novel by John

"No Matter Where You Go, Somebody's Been There Already"

Banville, the story's narrator Max Morden goes back to the seaside town of Ballyless, where he spent his childhood summer holidays, in the hopes of coping with the recent death of his wife Anna. As he returns to *The Cedars*, that grand estate where once the Grace family languished away their idle summers (he the poor interloper who was lucky enough to make the acquaintance of its more well-off renters), Max nearly expects the old place to be the same as it was those 50 summers earlier. In trying to recapture the past, for this, since Anna's death, is all he now seems able to function in, he says:

> *I had hoped for something definite of the Graces, no matter how small or seemingly insignificant, a faded photo, say, forgotten in a drawer, a lock of hair, or even a hair-pin, lodged between the floorboards, but there was nothing, nothing like that. No remembered atmosphere, either, to speak of. I suppose so many of the living passing through—it is a lodging house, after all—have worn away all traces of the dead.*

As I recently passed yet another twenty-something anniversary of ordination to the priesthood, I reflected on the wonder and beauty of that grand day in time. But with it always comes a gnawing tinge of sadness and disappointment. While to all appearances that long-awaited occasion could not have been celebrated more perfectly, it was slightly shy of "perfection," as two incredibly important people in my life and journey toward that day were missing—my maternal grandmother Emma, who I am sure prayed me all the way to the moment I rested under Bishop Garland's outstretched hands, and my dear friend Fr. Stan Cmich,

C.Pp.S., who died of cancer only six weeks beforehand, after serving as a priest for merely two years. Fr. Stan was to preach my first Mass in Pittsburgh the week following the ordination liturgy.

Fortunately for me, and for all of us who claim the name *Christian*, we are not condemned to suffer from *hotel syndrome* in our passing through this life. Rediscovering this spirit as I walked amongst the pueblo peoples of New Mexico, I was reaffirmed in my own faith tradition and teaching that there can be no illusion amongst Christians that no one has come before us and occupied our space (although, sometimes in our struggles and anguish, we feel as though we are the first ones in all of history undergoing some woeful tribulation).

In fact, as Max Morden's search illustrates, we desperately need to see, feel, experience, and be assured of traces of those who have gone before us, and who, in our longing desire, are with us still. To purge our spaces, whether physical, psychological, or emotional, of those who have been dear to us, is unthinkable. Rather, we seem to want to surround ourselves with memories, with touchstones of those who have since died, so that we might once again experience, albeit in a less than satisfactory way than we would greatly desire, their influence, presence, and love. We watch the well-trod steps we take so as not to "wear away" the traces of the dead.

No, unlike guests briefly "owning" and then passing through a hotel accommodation, leaving no trace behind (except for the credit card receipt), we are a people who leave our mark, want to be remembered, and know deep down that memory is our most significant stand against the passage of time's giant eraser.

And more than this, we have another destination, a destination where all traces of our lives will be permanently, indelibly

"No Matter Where You Go, Somebody's Been There Already"

marked in the heart of God for all eternity.

At times, in our busyness and inattentiveness, we the living, as we pass through the spaces of life once occupied by others, allow the traces of loved ones momentarily to slip away. And then something happens, something stirs inside us or around us, and the dead come back to life, and we once again touch them and their meaning for our lives, and we are deeply thankful, that in God's grand estate, God's many-roomed mansion, the *dead* are indeed living, so that we, the *living* can find our way home.

No matter where you go, somebody's been there already. I encourage you to spend some time recollecting those neglected *traces* left behind in your life that need remembering.

Life Lesson:

"If The Clay's Not Moist, You Can't Throw The Pot"

"IF THE CLAY'S NOT MOIST, YOU CAN'T THROW THE POT"

Many of the drawings of biblical events found in my very first *Golden Books Children's Bible* are still quite vivid in my imagination. In fact, this particular text is still sold today, and every once in a while, I'll wander through the children's section of the bookstore and grab hold of a copy, just to reminisce. I don't believe it has changed one bit since the time I treasured it as a child.

Perhaps my early fascination with the tale of Jacob's struggle with the angel, as related in the Book of Genesis (32:23-33), owes itself to the dramatic rendering of this divine-human encounter found in that bible. I can still see the figure of Jacob, biceps bulging, sandaled feet firmly planted in the desert dust, engaging in hand-to-hand combat with a mysterious heavenly emissary. Even though I was a child, I knew that angels worked for God, but somehow I imagined that Jacob should have prevailed in the tussle; after all, the angel's wings seemed to be getting in the way of wrestling Jacob to the ground! Somehow, I deemed angels to be sissies—what with their puffy feathers, flowing dresses, and their *Lilt* home permanent hairdos. Of course, as the story goes, Jacob indeed was prevailing...until the angel took a cheap shot and struck Jacob in the hip joint!

Now, I suppose from my present vantage point in life, it's not so much the biblical picture that keeps the story a fascination, but rather the reality of my own struggles with the divine. The wrestling match between Jacob and God (in the guise of a heavenly messenger) is incredibly human, incredibly believable because the struggles go on in the mind, heart and soul of every "Jacob" who lays claim to a relationship with God. We all can identify our own *Peniels* (the name Jacob gave to the place of his wrestling match), our own places of divine-human wrestling, where we have encountered *the face of God*—and also like Jacob, we have *lived to tell about it*. While perhaps not walking away from these encounters with a new name, as *Jacob-turned-Israel* did, we most likely have departed with a new perspective or new way of acting.

The struggle between Jacob and the man-turned-angel-turned-God is a classic rendition of an oft-repeated stage in the spiritual life. As we look back over our life stories, we can mark out many *Peniels* along the way, where we have witnessed the face of God—not only in pristine and glorious ways, but most certainly in ways that have wrenched, not our hip sockets, but rather our hearts and our minds. To draw intimate with God clearly means that we must wrestle with who God is, how we understand or do not understand God, and how we will respond to the divine One who mixes it up with us on the wrestling mat of daily life.

It seems that a recurrent stage of our spiritual journey is the struggle between our attempts to *shape* God and God's attempts to *shape us*.

I come to these reflections and life lesson because of my growing admiration of the art of Native American pottery. Much like the *writing* of Eastern Christian iconography, the crafting of Native American pottery is a spiritual exercise, as much the result of prayer as it is of practical skill. The role of spirituality in the

"If The Clay's Not Moist, You Can't Throw The Pot"

creation of pueblo pottery is significant.

The common thread that binds the individual characteristics, styles, coloration, and methods of the various Native potteries is the sense of emergence from the earth. Pottery, like most things in pueblo existence, emerges from and in concert with the great *circle of life*. A potter scrapes the clay from Mother Earth, brings the pot to life from the clay, and eventually returns the pot back to the earth so another generation can begin the process anew.

In a meditation written centuries ago by St. Irenaeus of Lyons, we find these challenging, yet moving words:

> *It is not you who shape God. It is God who shapes you. If then you are the work of God, await the hand of the Artist who does all things in due season. Offer him your heart, soft and tractable, and keep the form in which the Artist has fashioned you. Let the clay be moist, lest you grow hard and lose the imprint of his fingers.*

Every potter knows this life lesson emerging from their very hands and heart: **If the clay's not moist, you can't throw the pot.**

The images of Irenaeus quickly bring to mind a favorite Scripture passage of so many Christians, the story of the prophet Jeremiah and the potter. In Jeremiah 18:1-2,

The word that came to Jeremiah from the Lord: 'Come, go down to the potter's house, and there I will let you hear my words' (NRSV).

Jeremiah witnesses the potter working at the wheel, and the prophet ultimately comes to experience the revelation: Just *like the clay in the potter's hand, so are you in my hand, O house of Israel.*

While in many ways, the image is comforting and reassuring,

yet herein lays the struggle, the beginnings of the lifelong wrestling match we engage in with God. The potter is in control… the potter does all the shaping. But we want to be in control; we want to do our own fashioning and shaping. Native potter Rose Naranjo of the Santa Clara pueblo, speaking of the nature of the clay with which she works, says: *The clay is very selfish. It will form itself to what the clay wants to be.* Native American pottery crafters know all too well, the clay has a mind of its own!

In fact, when we witness the work of the potter at the wheel, while technique is everything, we also come to see that the clay doesn't always have the best of it! Witness a potter working, fashioning clay: the potter beats it, slaps it, roughs it up…the potter squeezes and pinches it…the potter mishandles and smashes it down, only to start up again. And then, of course, there's the constant *spinning*, the dizzy whirling and twirling of the wheel, nearly pulling the clay apart, if not for the steady hands of the potter holding it together. No, the life of the "clay" is not easy, compared with that of the potter.

Quite often, we are the ones who want to saddle up on the potter's stool; we want to be the ones doing the smashing and squeezing, the stretching and slapping, the pinching and pushing. We want to be the ones *shaping* God rather than being shaped *by* God.

I can recall quite vividly, in the days and weeks immediately following the September 11th attacks upon the people of the United States, how I found myself, perhaps not so vehemently as others more deeply wounded and scarred by that fateful day, but similarly nonetheless, wanting to shape God into an *avenger*. Clearly there is, as with any way of envisioning God, scriptural support for that very image. We want God to rise up and strike

"If The Clay's Not Moist, You Can't Throw The Pot"

down those who dishonor and kill the just and innocent. We long for a God whose actions echo those of the God of the Hebrews, wiping out those who stood in the way of God's chosen ones.

When faced with the grief and mourning of those who have lost loved ones in tragic death of any kind, I want God to be the God of Resurrection, not the God of Calvary. As I stand by helplessly with those whose tears won't stop flowing and whose faith is shattered in times of pain, disappointment and failure, I'm wrestling internally with a God whom I desperately want to take it all away *with mighty arm and outstretched hand.*

Upon stumbling into a moment of victory or success, at least as I may be judging or defining success in a particular effort of mine, I long for a God who brings many more such "victories," rather than a God who seemingly wants to send me more tests than triumphs.

When singing the beautiful refrain of a hymn that boldly proclaims, *The Lord hears the cry of the poor,* what I really want is to see the God who not only *hears* the cry of the poor, but rather who *does something about* their cries!

While listening to school children belting out these words during a weekday Mass, *The heavens are telling the glory of God,* in my mind's eye, I can't help but replay the sickening sight of the commercial airliner smashing into the World Trade Center, and the *heavens* filling with soot, twisted metal, and the remains of human beings. Without skipping a beat or betraying my inner thoughts, I am faced with a God whose *shape* I cannot quite embrace in the moment, but to whom I still have to give honor and glory as I preside over this Eucharistic liturgy.

I think…no, I am certain that I often struggle with *offering my heart, soft and tractable* to God as St. Irenaeus exhorts. I am the selfish clay Rose Naranjo tries to throw into a beautiful piece of pottery. This is too much vulnerability; this is too much risk. I see the *cross,* not a stunning piece of pottery, as the fate of those, who like Jesus himself, offer their entire heart and soul to the Father.

And the struggle continues, the wrestling goes on, but not with fluffy-white-winged angels plucked from the front of a Renaissance-style Christmas card, but rather with the stuff of life that pushes our human spirit, generosity, and sensibility to incredible limits.

Being the clay, allowing ourselves *to be moist* enough for God to fashion and shape, to throw this pot of ours is not easy. It is much easier to grow hardened, to dry out, and to remain intractable and non-malleable. Perhaps this is not what we would want or choose, for we don't seem to enjoy the effects of hardened hearts nor dried out souls, but we so easily become this less-than-moist clay when exposed to the elements, the conditions of the lives we live.

If the clay's not moist, you can't throw the pot. Being moist clay, however, is the only way in which we can allow God to be God! Being moist clay is the only way the Potter, the *Artist,* as Irenaeus calls God, can continue with God's labor of love, with the artistry of caring for humanity. Much like Dora Jody Folwell of Santa Clara pueblo says in describing the place from which her pottery art emanates, so too it is with God: *My pieces start out somewhere deep down inside me.* Our creation flows from the very depth of God's heart, the very unity of the Trinity and its divine *circle of life and love.*

Clearly there are things we can do, elements to which we can expose ourselves that will prevent us from drying out, from hardening to the point of uselessness. And, at the same time, there are

"If The Clay's Not Moist, You Can't Throw The Pot"

so many ways in which God sends water upon the parched and cracked surface of our clay, moistening us without any effort or work on our part, without any productivity or performance—simply as gift, simply as grace.

As moistened clay, I am once again prepared, albeit still with a tinge of reservation, to be open to God's firm but compassionate hands, as God shapes me rather than me shaping God.

My clay is moistened every time I witness young children, with their broad grins, plunking a few coins into the offering baskets during the procession of gifts at Sunday liturgy, sometimes waving to me as they pass by, quietly mouthing, "Hi, God!"

My clay is moistened and God is shaping me concerning my expectations whenever I receive a brief note in the mail that expresses gratitude for my ministry in the community and which pledges prayerful support for my leadership of service.

The dryness of my own disappointments and struggles to change is moistened when I take the time to listen to others who are making radical changes in their lives in order to continue to grow, or to escape debilitating relationships and addictions, or to reorient the priorities of their family life.

The harsh desire for an avenging God gives way to the *moist* experience of a God who moves people, after much pain and struggle, to offer forgiveness to the perpetrators of murder and rape. A softening occurs whenever people who have experienced incredible suffering and loss seek peace instead of vengeance.

In my own wrestling matches with a Church besieged with a lack of ordained clergy to minister the sacraments in full and meaningful ways, my clay is moistened as I listen to a young grade school boy dreaming about a career choice one day between being an architect…or being a priest.

As I wrestle with a God who seemingly refuses to be shaped by my rather infrequent requests for personal favors, my clay is moistened when my prayers are "answered," but in a way much richer, much more lasting than anything I ever asked for.

My clay is moistened when, in the midst of the dryness that can be born out of sometimes rigid, inflexible, boring, overly wordy, and convoluted rituals Sunday after Sunday, I witness a man, who upon finding the doors of the church locked after the last Sunday Mass, falling to his knees outside the locked church doors and offering his prayers to the God who shapes us.

Jacob thought he was getting the best of his heavenly challenger, but in the end, the divine wrestler had his way with Jacob. The clay is sometimes resistant, selfish to the artistry of the Potter, but in the end, the Potter has a way of fashioning and shaping as the Potter pleases. And even with full knowledge that the Artist's pots are not always thrown to perfection, the Potter won't destroy them. The Potter loves them as much as a perfect pot.

In the midst of the clay of our lives becoming dry, parched, cracked, intractable and hardened, the Divine Artist sends water, and we are once again moist enough to be smashed and squeezed, stretched and slapped, pinched and pushed into the beautiful, resplendent creations of a tender and loving and artful God.

If the clay's not moist, you can't throw the pot! What may be hardening, drying out your clay these days? In what ways have you been selfish, insistent clay rather than soft, malleable clay? How are you staying moist these days?

Perhaps no better or simpler prayer can rise from our lips in the coming days, as we echo the sentiments of St. Irenaeus, ***Lord, keep me moist!***

Life Lesson:

"Every Majestic, Soaring Mountain Springs From A Stressful Eruption Down Below"

"Every Majestic, Soaring Mountain Springs From A Stressful Eruption Down Below"

Making the 22-mile climb on West Highway 4 out of Jemez Springs, New Mexico, one eventually arrives at the *Valle Grande Caldera* National Preserve. It is a stunning sight to behold. Standing in the midst of its length and breadth, the world, and time, and your own life shrink to an infinitesimal grain.

This now 89,000 acre grassy bowl, 14 miles in diameter, is the largest volcanic *caldera* in the world. Formed over 1 million years ago (geological estimates put it between 1.3-1.5 million), a caldera is a cauldron-like (hence the name) feature formed by the collapse of land following a volcanic eruption. Over 1 million years ago, this volcano expelled more than 750 cubic kilometers of ash and lava.

As I stood perched on a lookout point in the midst of this gape-mouthed caldera, I realized that I was standing in what was once a massive cooking pot of lava. And what did this cauldron produce? Nothing less than these stunning Jemez Mountains, red rocks and tent rocks littering the landscape for miles! The highest point in the caldera is Redondo Peak, an 11,250' resurgent lava dome located entirely within the caldera. From the massive eruptions and collapses over time, breathtaking peaks soaring

"Every Majestic, Soaring Mountain Springs from a Stressful Eruption Down Below"

10-12,000 feet were given birth. Without these stressful eruptions long ago, there'd be no hypnotic landscape to scale today.

Every majestic, soaring mountain springs from a stressful eruption down below!

After basking in the glory of the scene, and surprisingly feeling not inconsequential, but rather relieved in the face of the history of this land and the passage of time that has come and gone since that initial eruption, I returned to my retreat lodge just beyond the village of Jemez Springs (content now to be lodging only at a 6,200' elevation).

Later that night, while immersed in the Gospel of John, I came upon a series of passages that planted the seeds for this life lesson:

> *And just as Moses lifted up the serpent in the wilderness, so must the Son of Man be lifted up, that whoever believes in him may have eternal life (NRSV John 3:14-15).*
>
> *So Jesus said, 'When you have lifted up the Son of Man, then you will realize that I am he, and that I do nothing on my own, but I speak these things as the Father instructed me (NRSV John 8: 28).*
>
> *And I, when am lifted up from the earth, will draw all people to myself (NRSV John 12:32).*

Only after the stressful eruption of his passion and death is Jesus lifted up so as to draw all people to himself. The "mount" of Calvary, from which Christ will reign even before the resurrection, breaks forth only after the eruption of his betrayal, torture, and condemnation.

And there are other scriptural mountains from which beauty emerges, but only after stressful eruptions down below. Moses' ascent of Mount Sinai and his meeting God face-to-face to receive the Law only comes after 40 years of wandering discontent and despair in the desert. The Transfiguration experience of Jesus atop that glorious mountain, in the presence of Peter, James and John (not to mention Elijah and Moses), is preceded by his prediction of his passion and death, and the truth that the cross is a condition of discipleship. The glory of Lazarus' emergence from the tomb (not a mountain per se, but a "mountainous" eruption) comes only after four days in the tomb. In fact, Jesus says earlier in John's account, "It is good that I wasn't here!" The truth is loud and clear: only after the stressful eruption of loss and pain and disappointment comes the rising to new life.

And how many times is this life lesson truth for us? I remember my first days as a priest, starting my ministry at St. Joseph's College, Rensselaer, Indiana, the very college I had graduated from a mere 5 years before. In the trepidation of beginning my life as a priest, in a ministry I had not specifically prepared for, arriving under stressful changes in the department only a month before, trying to be the colleague rather than the student of men and women who were my revered teachers only a short time ago—I happened to meet someone who was to become a life-long friend. But it was a relationship that began from our stressful eruptions!

Frank arrived on campus as a newly minted freshman quarterback for the Puma football team, and he landed in the residence hall room right across from my paltry little apartment (and calling it an "apartment" is quite benevolent on my part). For some odd reason, his roommate, a fellow football prospect, never

"Every Majestic, Soaring Mountain Springs from a Stressful Eruption Down Below"

showed on campus, and even more surprisingly, Frank was able to keep the room as a single the whole year. As we both meandered through our first year triumphs and defeats (and everything else in between), Frank struggled with his place on the football team. Eventually, late in the second semester, just as spring football workouts were coming to a close, Frank was informed that his scholarship money had been withdrawn, and that he would have to navigate the pricey cost of Catholic private education on his own. It was painful for Frank and me to see this development, but I felt sure he could return to St. Joseph's in the fall and begin anew with a different hope and dream.

While visiting Frank and his family during the summer months, he delivered the news to me that he was unable to get the loans and funding together to continue his education at St. Joseph's and would be moving to a junior college close to home, with a small scholarship to once again take a shot at football quarterbacking. I was incredibly sad at the news, and although I didn't speak the words, I believed this meant the end of our budding friendship—after all, in the course of life as we know it, even the 90 mile distance between Rensselaer, IN and Elmwood Park, IL might as well have been a trip to Europe! Distance doesn't always treat even the most stable relationships well, sometimes even when that distance might be the other side of town.

But here, 27 years later, the friendship continues and prospers, despite a recent move by Frank and his wife to London, England! I share this story because it is one illustration of a wonderful gift of life that grew not only from those eruptions in the early days of college life, but has weathered additional stressful eruptions through the intervening years.

When I reflect upon the invitation extended by God to Mary

of Nazareth to be the mother of Jesus, the Mother of God, I quickly realize that long before the "majesty and soaring" entrance of the Word Made Flesh at the Incarnation, there were indeed numerous stressful eruptions (just read Matthew and Luke). And clearly more were to follow. The prophet Simeon, on the day Jesus was presented by his parents at the temple, blessed the couple and spoke to Mary: *This child is destined for the falling and the rising of many in Israel, and to be a sign that will be opposed so that the inner thoughts of many will be revealed—and a sword will pierce your own soul, too (NRSV Luke 2:34-35).*

Birthing is a joyful, wondrous, majestic event, yet it is wrought with pain and difficulty. Birthing is still a dangerous and stressful undertaking; no wonder it's called *labor*. Birthing is exhausting, draining, and always leaves scars, even ones that are not immediately available to the eye. The great medieval German mystic Meister Eckhart once wrote these profound words: *We are all called to be 'Mothers of God,' for God is always needing to be born.*

What is being birthed in your life at this moment? What labor are you enduring in order to see a spark of majesty, of soaring abundant life emerge? What eruptions are percolating below the surface of your job, your relationships, your prayer life, your commitments, your visions and dreams? Are you frightened by these stresses? Are you concocting schemes to squash these eruptions, or to tame them?

Heed the words of the Letter to the Romans:

> *I consider that the sufferings of this present time are not worth comparing with the glory about to be revealed to us. For the creation waits with eager longing for the revealing of the children of God. We know that*

"Every Majestic, Soaring Mountain Springs From A Stressful Eruption Down Below"

the whole creation has been groaning in labor pains until now; and not only the creation, but we ourselves, who have the first fruits of the Spirit, groan inwardly while we wait for adoption, the redemption of our bodies. Likewise, the Spirit helps us in our weakness; for we do not know how to pray as we ought, but that very Spirit intercedes with sighs too deep for words (NRSV Romans 8: 18-19.22-24.26).

Whether it be the magnificent peaks of Redondo and the Valle Grande Caldera, or the lava percolating beneath the surface of each of our lives and the life of all creation, the truth of this life lesson is clear: **Every majestic, soaring mountain always starts from some stressful eruption down below.**

Beyond The Land Of Enchantment!
LIVING THE LESSONS EVERY DAY

"It would be lovely if the places you visited opened you up, made you more aware, startled you and made you reflect on how much you loved home."
(Barry Lopez)

While Waiting For My Baggage To Come

Standing in the baggage area at Orlando International last night at 11pm, the only thing I could think about was "getting home." Although I had just returned from a wonderfully relaxing trip to one of my favorite parts of the country, where the weather was very un-Florida-like, the mountains were glistening in the sun, and the cooling breezes were beginning to rustle the golden leaves of the aspens and cottonwoods, I still was anxious to end a long travel day and climb back into my own bed.

Of course, the arrival of the baggage never cooperates with our timetables for getting on our way home, and so like many others, including two parishioners who traveled on the same flight (they left earlier than me, though), we waited…and waited…and waited. As is normally the case, we all stood there watching the same one or two pieces of luggage make their way along the squeaking, clacking conveyor belt, wondering who they belonged to, and eerily hoping that if we stared at them long enough, maybe they would morph into our own bags! As the crowd got more exasperated (lots of huffing and puffing, as well as tales being spun about the last time someone didn't received their luggage—always an incendiary thing to talk about with other angry passengers), I began to think I would have been satisfied to take either of those two pieces of endlessly rotating anonymous luggage—just to get out of the airport!

In my wandering mind, already lagging because of time zone changes, I began to think about how our lives are sometimes just like those two lonely pieces of unclaimed baggage, charting the same trail over and over and over again. And like the waiting passengers, we keep looking for something more, something surprising to pop out of that mysterious opening, something we really desire—but far too frequently, we all get stuck watching the same things passing us by, snaking along our own little repetitive paths.

This is why, I believe, God sends us **prophets**. Whether in the Old Testament or in the person of Jesus Christ, or in any time throughout history, including our own, prophets are sent by God to bump us off the treadmill, to open us to the incredible variety of ways in which God comes to us, speaks to us, and touches us.

In order to do this, however, prophets always need to pull us, to stretch us, to move us off the usual, repetitive paths we *choose* to get stuck on—and they invite us into new ways of seeing, hearing, and experiencing God. Perhaps this is why prophets, when they first confront us, scratch us the wrong way, get under our skin, and make us a bit queasy. A scripture scholar once described prophets as "people whose message we *do not want* to hear—but whose message we *absolutely need* to hear"!

But because we are human, it seems to be in our nature to get stuck (and stay stuck), to become stale, and to only want things to happen the way *we want* them to and *expect* them to happen.

Some of the great figures of salvation history demonstrate the same problem—so we are in good company. In the Book of Numbers chapter 11, God pours out God's powerful spirit upon seventy elders, sharing with them some of the same gifts Moses himself received from God. That spirit was so mighty that even two men, not present with the assembled seventy others, also were able to receive the gifts of God. And what was the response of the people to this great generosity of God? They complained, were jealous, and couldn't believe that God would be so *liberal* in the way God's gifts were dished out.

Jesus' apostles, in the Gospel of Mark chapter 9, were no better. John speaks up for the rest of the apostles when he learns that someone, not part of their chosen apostolic group, was driving out demons and healing in Jesus' name. Again, the tone is one of anger and indignation. In a sense, John was saying—how dare God share God's healing power with people who are not with the "in" group—after all, what's the value of being "in" when it ends up that just anyone can come along and reap the rewards?

On occasion, indeed many of us are infected with this very human virus. We get stuck; often we can only see and hear and experience God in one way—and then we expect God to honor that one way of reaching us. And when we do in fact encounter God coming in ways with which we are not familiar, in people and situations we usually avoid, in circumstances that shake our comforts—we too can become jealous, angry, defensive, confused, and like the elder son in the parable of the Prodigal Son, we can even become bitter about God's lavish generosity.

We seem to always want to *limit* the God who is always *beyond* any limits we imagine, create, or impose.

As Moses tells the people in the Book of Numbers…and the living Word of God pierces our present day hearts: **"Would that all the people of the Lord were prophets!"**

Would that each of us could *find the prophet* who will pull us off that endless, repetitive treadmill where the same baggage keeps passing by until we are sick of looking at it.

Would that each of us could *become a prophet*, a person who will pull, and stretch, and move others to see, and hear, and experience God in new and marvelous ways!

In the end, of which there never really is any in the *circle* of life, there is always the return from a journey. In the words of poet T. S. Eliot, we return to the place where we started, but in the hope of *knowing it for the first time*. And hopefully, if that journey has been fruitful, there will be something in our baggage that wasn't there before we set out (and perhaps something left behind at our departure that we took with us when we began). Now, I'm not thinking about those trinkets we often carry home to loved ones so they don't feel neglected, but rather treasures for our own well-being.

This has been, and continues to be my hope and prayer for everyone who undertakes the journey through these life lessons from *The Land of Enchantment*. May there be a voice *tucked in the rocks* beckoning you to more abundant life.

Postscript

*"Do I presume to touch
The divine
And squeeze
From this limping soul
A spark and light
To flame and kindle others?"
(Denise Levertov, "Reluctant Writer")*

Ah yes, a "reluctant writer"—aren't we all who dive into the power of words and dare to construct sentences that reach beyond our private notebooks and journals? For so many years, I kept the bulk of my writing, except for required theology school assignments and theses, to myself. I kept running into a brick wall with this larger than life sentiment spray painted on it by the graffiti critic buried in my head: "DON'T YOU DARE! YOU HAVE NOTHING *ORIGINAL* TO SAY!" I often wondered, what's the point of writing (or saying) all this since it's not *original*? Somehow I equated the mysterious quality of *originality* with relevance.

Then a turning point came. I began to recognize that even though my own writing is torn from the pages of others' thoughts, works and reflections, it is I, not *they*, who bring something new to life in the way I arrange, rearrange, and share my own life experiences through the prism of those whose words live inside me. The *originality*, if that is even the right word, rests in the way the words and experiences move through me and eventually emerge in speech or on paper.

A fine poet, novelist, and short story writer, with whom I share a friendship, once explained during a book club discussion how characters and stories came to life in his own writing process. He illustrated the process by explaining how three particular scenes in one of his short stories had a foundation in reality, i.e. they were *true* events, but ones that had occurred at different times, periods of life, locations and circumstances. At some point, however, they became slightly altered in order to fit the current plot of this or that short story. He referred to these recollected events and characters as threads or strands, which then get rewoven into a new context, a new story that has its own life apart from, yet connected to, the original people, places and circumstances.

It seems to me this is not only how writing comes to birth, but how our life is lived! So many threads, strands, and pieces occur over time in our lives (most of which we are no longer fully conscious of), and then we try to make something of these threads—weave them together in a story, *our* story, so we can make sense of who we are, where we've come from, and where we may be heading. We connect, disconnect, reconnect the pieces as we go along, finding some threads more necessary at times than others—some perhaps more colorful, warm, revelatory, soothing, disturbing—and we weave them into a narrative by which we attempt to navigate our daily lives.

Sometimes, as in a worn piece of clothing, strands come loose, dangle, stick out, become annoying—and in doing so, they catch our attention in a peculiar way. We then have to be careful as to what we do with them. Sometimes pulling here or there, even gently, leads to a necessary, but messy unraveling and repair.

These *Life Lessons from the Land of Enchantment*, tucked in the rocks amidst the spectacular New Mexican landscape, are testimony to this process of writing and life. They are strands and threads, drawn from various times and places, that have coalesced into what you have now read on these pages. They are *original* in so far as they are reflected through the prism of my life and vision. As Ojibway elder Blackwolf Jones has written in *Listen to the Drum*:

> *Hear your own heartbeat. Put your ear to your own heart and listen with a sharp ear.*

What you share with me in these pages is the fruit of this wise advice, and I hope that these words continue to be for you an invitation to do the same. I pray this effort creates a kind of *spiritual communion* between this writer and you, and more importantly, between you and the Author of Life!

> *"In the end we are what we remember and what we imagine—nothing more. We tend to remember those moments when we are most intensely alive, whether with pain or joy. We search for a common language that would bind writer and reader together in a spiritual communion."*
> *(David M. Johnson, Rebirth of Wonder: Poems of the Common Life, 2007)*

CPSIA information can be obtained at www.ICGtesting.com
Printed in the USA
LVOW010826010213

317959LV00001B/5/P